INSIGHT COMPACT GUIDES

Snowdonia

N

GW00370456

Compact Guide: Snowdonia is the ideal quick-reference guide to this extraordinarily varied part of Wales. It tells you all you need to know about Snowdonia's attractions, from rugged mountains, deep cwms, dark forests and glorious coastlines to ancient sites, medieval castles, slate caverns and Great Little Trains.

This is one of almost 100 titles in *Apa Publications'* acclaimed series of pocket-sized, easy-to-use guidebooks intended for the independent-minded traveller. *Compact Guides* are in essence travel encyclopedias in miniature, designed to be comprehensive yet portable, as well as up-to-date and authoritative.

PARC CENEDLAETHOL ERYRI

SNOWDONIA
NATIONAL PARK

Star Attractions

An instant reference to some of Snowdonia's top attractions to help you set your priorities.

Conwy p15

Ffestiniog Railway p27

Slate caverns p28

Caernarfon p33

Snowdon p35

Lleyn Peninsula p37

Portmeirion p41

Harlech p43

Centre for Alternative Technology p51

Coed-y-Brenin p53

Celtica p59

Snowdonia
NORTH WALES

Introduction

Places

Culture

Leisure

Practical Information

Snowdonia – Place of Eagles

Opposite: Welsh Black cattle and Birds' Rock

Snowdonia's dramatic array of mountain peaks and valleys contains the highest and some of the wildest land south of the Scottish border. It is known to the Welsh as *Eryri*, 'Place of Eagles'. When the traveller and essayist George Borrow toured North Wales in 1854, he wrote of it: 'Perhaps in all the world there is no region more picturesquely beautiful.' A bold claim yet one not hard to justify. Elsewhere there may be loftier mountains, deeper lakes, greater forests and swifter rivers but rarely are they found in such unique combinations, lit and watered by Atlantic weather.

Today, while Welsh Black cattle and the ubiquitous Welsh Mountain sheep share their hillsides with walkers and cyclists, climbers and hang-gliders, farming continues much as it has for generations. The common place name *hafod* (or *hafotty*) meaning 'summer dwelling' recalls the old tradition of transhumance when stock were moved to higher pastures during the warmer months. Drystone walls snaking over ridge and summit date from the 18th and 19th centuries, separating valley from *ffridd* (mountain pasture), one farm from the next.

The Dolgoch Falls

Much of Snowdonia's earlier prosperity rested upon that impervious, blue-grey stone that splits so conveniently into flat sheets. Long-abandoned slate quarries may still scar many a mountainside but their narrow-gauge railways and workings have long become visitor attractions in their own right. Other much older sites reach back through layers of history, none more evocatively than the great coastal fortresses built during Edward I's 30-year subjugation of the Welsh in the 13th century.

It has been said that people will visit Cumbria for its lakes, but Wales for its mountains. Eryri's peaks are, indeed, a thrilling presence: inspirational to explore by road, challenging to those who walk and climb. The great crags and gullies have become associated with Britain's best known rock-climbers and mountaineers. Equally deserving, though often less well publicised, is Snowdonia's glorious coastline stretching north from the Dovey estuary round the Lleyn Peninsula and Anglesey to the River Conwy. Nowhere else in Britain are high mountains and splendid seaside found in such close proximity.

5

All aboard the Ffestiniog Railway

Location and topography

Snowdonia National Park was designated in 1951. Occupying some 838 square miles (217,100 hectares) of Northwest Wales, it is Britain's second largest national park after the Lake District. Several mountain ranges fall within its boundary, including all Wales's 14 summits over 3000ft

A winter ascent

Glasllyn on Snowdon

Summer sun on Anglesey

6

(914m), as well as broad tracts of moorland and forest. The area's eastern fringe runs in a line from the Vale of Conwy to Bala, Dinas Mawddwy and Machynlleth. The most frequently climbed peaks are Snowdon ('Yr Wyddfa') in the north and Cadair Idris in the south. Although lying outside the national park perimeter itself, both the Lleyn Peninsula and Anglesey are considered scenically, culturally and historically part of the region.

Igneous rock along with volcanic ashes, lavas and shales from the Ordovician Period make up much of the savagely beautiful geology around Snowdon and Cadair Idris. Older Cambrian rocks are most evident in the mountains of the Harlech Dome bordering Tremadog Bay. But by far the most striking influence on the entire Snowdonia landscape has been that of glacial ice.

The Ice Age which began some 2 million years ago and ended around 10,000 years ago has left an extraordinary and highly visible legacy in Snowdonia. At times throughout that period of very cold climate cycles, great ice sheets thousands of feet thick spread from Scandinavia to Britain, enveloping the seas and lowlands as far south as the English Channel. Meanwhile, permanent accumulations of snow on higher ground spawned glaciers which slowly but inexorably flowed downhill, grinding away the bedrock, smoothing out 'U'-shaped valleys and depositing huge mounds of excavated material we call moraines. Steeply hollowed basins known in Wales as *cwms,* usually filled by lakes and surrounded by cliffs, were left behind in higher locations by the retreating ice. In geological terms 10,000 years is merely the blink of an eye, too brief a time for significant weathering to have taken place. The result is a mountain landscape little changed since the last glacier melted.

Climate

Hills and mountains create their own weather. In common with most of upland Britain lying in the path of the prevailing westerly winds, there is greater rainfall (snow in winter) here than over the adjacent lowlands. More than 185in (4,700mm) of precipitation have been recorded on the Snowdonia mountains in one year and even in a drought year 100in (2,540mm) is not uncommon. Temperature falls as altitude is gained – about 3°C (5°F) for every 1,000ft (300m). Snow often lingers on north-facing slopes above 2,000ft (600m) well into May. Winds are notoriously fickle, sometimes funnelling viciously through valleys and over passes, at other times disappearing altogether in sheltered locations.

Snowdonia's climate – essentially a collection of mini-climates – is changeable throughout the year, with the best of the weather usually, though not always, to be found

Pedal power at Pen-y-Pass

on the fringes of the hills. Higher villages and roads may be shrouded in mist for days on end while those in the lee of high ground bask in sunshine. In westerly or south-westerly weather, districts such as the Vale of Conwy and the North Coast are often fine while the West Coast and most of the mountains sulk under cloud and rain. Similarly, east winds produce favourable conditions over Anglesey and the Lleyn. The large central block of uplands, however, is less likely to benefit from this effect.

May, June and September are the driest months in an average year.

7

Welsh language and heritage

Beneath its veneer of tourism, Snowdonia is a stronghold of Welsh culture and tradition where one of Europe's oldest languages may be heard in everyday use. Much of the region's commerce and administration is undertaken in Welsh, most schools and road signs are bilingual and there are Welsh TV and radio channels. Welsh is the native tongue of around 65 per cent of the population.

Flag waving

Welsh belongs to the Celtic family of languages and is closely related to Cornish and Breton. Its origins stem from the Celtic Iron Age people who moved into Wales from the continent between about 550BC and AD50. Although the language was almost certainly being spoken as early as the 6th century AD, some of the first examples of written Welsh occur in tales from the *Mabinogion* dating from the 12th century or before.

Early Christianity:
St Cadfan's Stone at Tywyn

Christianity in Wales flourished throughout the Dark Ages. Missionary saints, among them St Beuno, St Cadfan and St Tudno, established cells in North Wales and Bardsey Island became a special place of pilgrimage for many centuries. The people of North Wales, united against raids initially by Anglo-Saxons and later by Norsemen, founded the Kingdom of Gwynedd under Rhodri Mawr,

Llywelyn in Conwy

their first great leader. The legendary hero Arthur appears to date from around this time, as do King Vortigen and Merlin the wizard. They figure prominently in the *Mabinogion*, a collection of folk tales drawn partly from the imagination of the Celtic bards and partly from quasi-historical events. The *Mabinogion* was first translated into English in 1838 and is now available in very readable form.

Between the 9th and 13th centuries came a great era of Welsh Princes, culminating in the reign of Llywelyn the Great. Tolerated at first by England's Norman kings, they were finally subdued by Edward I in his campaigns of 1276–7. His massive castles (at Conwy, Beaumaris, Caernarfon and Harlech, also at Fflint and Aberystwyth) bear testimony to the scale of the Anglo-Welsh conflict at that time. In the early 1400s Welsh hopes for independence rose with a rebellion under the famous Owain Glyndwr but when an Anglesey man – Henry Tudor – gained accession to the English throne in 1485 as Henry VII, Welsh loyalties seem to have turned.

Welshness permeates Snowdonia. Its geographical isolation has always encouraged self-reliance and an almost tribal sense of identity. Even today the people who live here can seem guarded, sometimes reticent with strangers. Despite increasing integration into a global community (or perhaps because of it), they remain fiercely proud of their Welsh roots.

Economy

Earning a living from the land in the rugged heart of Snowdonia has never been easy. Only the hardy Welsh Mountain sheep and Welsh Black cattle are able to withstand the harsh climate and convert rough grazing into profit for the farmer. Lambing extends from March well into April, after which each ewe and lamb will be driven up the hillside to range over its acre or so of ground. Shearing takes place during June and July. In September the flock is collected in lower fields where the female lambs are separated off to overwinter on kinder pastures such as those of Anglesey. Most male lambs are destined for slaughter. Older ewes run with the rams towards the end of October and thus the breeding cycle starts afresh.

Aspects of local farming

While traditional agriculture continues in the more fertile valleys and lowland fringes, forestry and electricity generation (both hydro and nuclear) contribute their share of regional income. Manufacturing industries too, including high-tech and independent television production companies, play an important role in the economy. This influx of enterprise has been encouraged by the opening of the A55 North Wales Coast Expressway. Its tunnels beneath the River Conwy and through rocky headlands represent one of Britain's largest civil engineering projects.

The scenic North Wales Coast railway forms part of the Euston to Holyhead line for the ferry services to Ireland. More lovely still is the single-track branch from Llandudno Junction to Blaenau Ffestiniog which threads the Vale of Conwy, providing a thrice-daily service for out-of-the-way villages. To the south, the Cambrian Coast Line connects with services east to the Midlands.

Blaenau Ffestiniog terminus

Sea fishing for mackerel, plaice, whiting and dab, here as throughout the UK, has suffered a steady decline and fishing boats no longer crowd the quaysides of little ports all round the coast from Aberdovey to Conwy as they once did. Conwy estuary mussels, however, remain in demand for local restaurants. The once important slate-mining industry faded in the late 1800s, leaving open wounds on the mountain landscape, particularly around Blaenau Ffestiniog, Bethesda and Llanberis. But high-quality slates are still produced in limited quantities.

With improved transport links from the Midlands and the North West, Snowdonia is welcoming ever more visitors. Many head for the hills and coast to walk, rock-climb, cycle, pony-trek, fish, sail or simply enjoy the scenery. Visitor attractions abound, from slate caverns and 'Great Little Trains' to historic buildings, farm parks, forest trails and museums. Increasingly the local economy depends upon income generated from these sources and the service industries associated with tourism in general.

Wildlife

Snowdonia's grazing sheep keep many upland plant species in check, but in high, steep locations so-called 'arctic alpines' flourish. There is one special flower that grows nowhere else in Britain except on inaccessible ledges in the Glyder and Snowdon ranges – the delicate Snowdon Lily. Elsewhere, limestone country and coastal dune systems support their own distinctive flora, among them orchids and the rare dune helleborine.

Lilies on Bearded Lake

Crags echo to the '*pruk pruk*' call of ravens and the buzzard's plaintive mewing. There are hovering kestrels, dashing sparrowhawks and red-billed choughs that sometimes nest in disused copper mines. Snowdonia's lakes, its saltmarshes and river estuaries attract all manner of water-loving and wading species. The sea cliffs of Anglesey, the Lleyn Peninsula and the offshore islands are home to large numbers of seabirds as well as to colonies of Atlantic grey seals.

Small mammals and birds abound in broadleaved woodland, including rarer insect-eating birds like the pied flycatcher. Oak acorns sustain jays, squirrels, mice and voles, the latter prey to tawny owls. Songbirds often colonise younger conifer plantations, though the region's established commercial forests generally contain less wildlife.

Historical Highlights

10,000BC With the ending of the Ice Age the glaciers retreat, though for many centuries tributary glaciers remain high up on valley walls. The mountains are hostile to man, valleys are densely forested and swift-flowing rivers hamper travel by foot. Anglesey is joined to the mainland until eventually separated by rising sea levels.

4,000BC Neolithic (Stone Age) people drift northwards along the European coast. They introduce primitive agriculture and the domestication of livestock. Their dead are buried in communal chambered tombs. A thriving 'axe factory' is developed on hills above Penmaenmawr.

2,000BC 'Beaker Folk' move westward from the continent, heralding the Bronze Age. They bring pottery and build stone circles.

400–500BC Iron Age Celts from central Europe spread north to Wales, introducing the origins of the Welsh language. The Druids, who preach immortality through rebirth and sometimes practise human sacrifice, have a strong power base on Anglesey. St Cadfan establishes a monastery on Bardsey Island which thereafter becomes an important pilgrimage destination.

AD61–80 The Romans attack North Wales and Anglesey from their legionary fortress at Deva (Chester). The Druids are exterminated.

400–500 As the Romans withdraw from Britain, Irish pirates attack the Welsh coast, followed by an influx of Irish settlers who bring Christianity with them. They are eventually overcome by the native Welsh under the leadership of Cunedda whose descendants establish their headquarters at Deganwy on the River Conwy.

784 Offa, greatest of all the Mercian kings, constructs a dyke along the Welsh-English border from Prestatyn to Chepstow. The people of the mountainous west call themselves *Cymry*, 'fellow-countrymen', hence *Cymru* for Wales.

800–900 North Wales suffers savage raids by the Vikings who are only prevented from lasting colonisation of the region by the leadership of Rhodri Mawr – Roderick the Great of Gwynedd, ruler of all Wales.

1188 Giraldus Cambrensis (Gerald of Barry), scholar, monk and son of a Norman settler, tours Wales with Archbishop Baldwin seeking recruits for the Third Crusade. He writes in his *Itinerary of Wales* of a poor people with a love of poetry and music and a natural gift for singing in harmony.

1194 Llywelyn ap Iorwerth (Llywelyn the Great) becomes Prince of Gwynedd, the most powerful Welsh ruler since the Norman invasion. After a life devoted to securing the territorial integrity of Wales he enters the monastery of Aberconwy in 1238 and dies two years later.

1255 Llywelyn the Great's grandson, Llywelyn ap Gruffydd (Llywelyn the Last) begins a campaign to rid Gwynedd of all the English and to establish his own authority as Prince of Wales. He misjudges the new spirit in England, refusing to pay homage to Edward I.

1277 Edward launches his attack upon the unruly Welsh by building fortresses backed by seapower. Llywelyn, forced to relinquish almost all his land, conspires for revenge with brother Dafydd.

1282–4 Edward extends his line of castles, takes Anglesey (the 'granary of Wales') and forces Llywelyn back into the mountains to be killed in a skirmish to the south at Cilmeri. Dafydd is captured and executed. All serious hopes for an independent Wales are ended. Edward's son, who would become notoriously irresponsible in later life, is born at Caernarfon Castle in 1284, the first English Prince of Wales.

1300–1400 Quasi-historical, romanticised Bardic legends of Wales are recorded in the *Mabinogion*.

1400–12 The Welsh rebel under their great hero Owain Glyndwr, initiating a struggle that would last nearly 14 years. Glyndwr holds parliaments at Machynlleth, Dolgellau and Harlech and forges alliances with the Scots, the Irish and the French. But Henry IV proves too strong and by 1412 Glyndwr is forced to live as an outlaw, dying four years later in an unknown hiding-place.

1485 Henry Tudor of Penmynydd on Anglesey becomes Henry VII of England.

1500–1600 The peasantry of North Wales remain impoverished. Cattle and cloth are produced but the region's great mineral wealth lies largely untouched. William Morgan, vicar of Llanrhaeadr-ym-Mochnant and later Bishop of Llandaff, translates the Bible into Welsh in 1588.

1768 Rich copper-ore deposits are found at Parys Mountain on Anglesey, provoking the rapid growth of nearby Amlwch from a fishing hamlet of six dwellings to a thriving, if rather unruly, boom town. A few years later copper ore is discovered high under Snowdon's summit; it is humped on men's backs 1,000ft (300m) over the top then sent by horse-drawn sledge down to the Saracen's Head by Llyn Cwellyn (now the Snowdon Ranger Track) and thence to Caernarfon docks. Thirty years on, a new road would be built through the Llanberis Pass.

1774 In the Introduction to his *A Tour through Wales and Monmouthshire*, H.P. Wyndham writes: '...while the English roads are crowded with travelling parties of pleasure, the Welsh are so rarely visited that the author did not meet with a single party during his six weeks' journey through Wales...' Travellers of the time are initially deterred by the Welsh language and the haunting unease of the wild mountains, though this will soon change.

1780–1800 Methodism spreads through North Wales. Thomas Charles of Bala, a leading influence, founds the British and Foreign Bible Society. In 1789 an *eisteddfod* at Corwen marks the rebirth of these traditional bardic festivals.

1815–30 Thomas Telford extends his turnpike road from London through Snowdonia, ending at Holyhead's Admiralty Arch. In 1826 he completes the revolutionary Menai Suspension Bridge.

1840 Richard Pennant who developed the vast Penrhyn slate quarries, the world's biggest opencast system, moves into Penrhyn Castle, an extravagant neo-Norman edifice designed by the fashionable architect, Thomas Hopper. Pennant's immense wealth from slate contrasts starkly with the hard, poorly paid lives of his employees.

1844 Gold is discovered at lead mines near Dolgellau and within 20 years a gold rush is under way. Most of the 130,000 ounces of gold extracted over the ensuing 60 years comes from just two mines – Clogau and Gwynfynydd, both situated near the banks of the Afon Mawddach.

1850 Robert Stephenson's tubular Britannia Bridge over the Menai Strait is opened, carrying the Chester to Holyhead railway. Anglesey's former dependence on ferry crossings to and from the mainland is finally ended.

1858 George Borrow, traveller, linguist and author from East Anglia, tours Wales with his stepdaughter. His well-known book *Wild Wales* is published in 1862, providing a rich, if flowery, picture of social conditions at the time.

1890 David Lloyd George from Llanystumdwy, near Criccieth, is elected Liberal Member of Parliament for Caernarfon Boroughs and goes on to lead Britain through World War I.

1950–60 Climbers Joe Brown and Don Whillans pioneer new routes, establishing North Wales as a major venue in the development of British rock-climbing. Following the first ascent of Everest in 1953, Plas y Brenin Outdoor Centre opens at Capel Curig.

1951 Snowdonia becomes a National Park.

1955 'C' Flight of Number 22 Search and Rescue Helicopter Squadron arrives at R.A.F. Valley on Anglesey. Teams are often called out to help walkers, climbers, swimmers and yachtsmen.

1969 Prince Charles is invested as Prince of Wales at a ceremony in Caernarfon Castle.

1971 The Welsh branch of the Search and Rescue Dog Association (SARDA) is formed. Its purpose is to speed up the rescue of people missing on the mountains and moors.

1996 Local government reorganisation creates a new Unitary Authority – Conwy – from the former Aberconwy and Colwyn borough council.

1997 In a referendum on devolution, the Welsh narrowly vote to set up a Welsh Assembly in Cardiff by 1999 with very limited powers.

The Carneddau from near Llyn Cwn, above the Devil's Kitchen

Route 1

The North Coast and Carneddau Mountains

Llandudno – Conwy – Betws-y-Coed – Capel Curig – Llyn Ogwen – Bethesda – Sychnant Pass (53 miles/85km) *See map on page 17*

Climbing on the Idwal Slabs

In his famous *Tour in Wales* published in 1778, Thomas Pennant found the Carneddau mountains 'very disagreeable, of dreary bottoms or moory hills...' Tastes change and many hillgoers now choose these sprawling whalebacks to escape the crowds on Snowdon and other popular peaks. The highest summit – Carnedd Llewelyn, 3,491ft (1,064m) – stands a mere 69ft (21m) lower than Snowdon itself. Carneddau means 'place of stones, or cairns', but while this describes the terrain here and there, grass predominates, swathing the vast ridges and cwms. Few roads penetrate far into these remote northernmost hills of Snowdonia, yet on every side they are bounded by scenery of extraordinary contrasts.

To the east lies the beautiful Vale of Conwy, a gentle landscape of fields and woodland leading to the darker conifers of Gwydir Forest and tumbling rivers around Betws-y-Coed. To the south the Carneddau mountains end where the rugged Glyder range begins at the dramatic Ogwen Valley, threaded by Telford's London to Holyhead turnpike highway, now the A5. The foothills overlooking Anglesey and Conwy Bay are too steep for the coast road and railway line which have been squeezed into a narrow corridor above the shore, tunnelling through headlands. Further north the Carneddau mountains drop abruptly to the Conwy estuary from where they often appear aloof, brooding, inaccessible.

Preceding pages: life at the top, Cadair Idris in the background

But we start at the coast. **Llandudno**'s reputation as one of Britain's finest Victorian seaside resorts is well founded. The town (pop. 20,000) was developed to a grid pattern on reclaimed marshland in the mid-1900s by Edward Mostyn and Owen Williams. Today grand hotels fronted by a broad promenade sweep round North Shore to the splendid ★ **Pier** without an entertainments arcade or fast-food outlet in sight.

The town's early success prompted entrepreneurs to construct **Marine Drive**, a toll road encircling the **Great Orme** limestone headland which now incorporates a ★ **Bronze Age Copper Mine** (underground tours February to end-October, daily 10am–5pm). In 1902 a ★ **Tramway** (Easter to October, daily 10am–5pm) was laid to the Great Orme's 680ft (207m) summit, complemented more recently hy a **Cabin Lift** (daily Easter to October, weather permitting), the longest in Britain. To savour this magnificent headland, walk round the perimeter wall from the car park, a distance of about 2 miles (3km); there are wide views over the Conwy estuary to distant Anglesey, the Carneddau mountains and even the Isle of Man. The Church of St Tudno, after whom the town is named, sits in a hollow overlooking the North Wales coast.

Llandudno pier and the view from Great Orme

Across Llandudno's isthmus on **West Shore** stands the White Rabbit statue commemorating the town's association with Lewis Carroll (alias the Rev. Charles Dodgson). He was a frequent guest of the Liddell family whose daughter, Alice, accompanied him on seashore walks and may have inspired the creation of his famous storybook character. See the **Alice in Wonderland Centre** in Trinity Square (daily except winter Sundays, 10am–4pm). There are flowery walks through **Haulfre** and **Happy Valley** gardens, a dry-ski slope and toboggan run, art exhibitions at **Oriel Mostyn** (daily except Sundays, 10am–5pm) and prestigious productions at the new **North Wales Theatre** on the seafront.

Leave Llandudno on the A546, shadowing the River Conwy's eastern shore to Deganwy and follow signs for Conwy, crossing the A55 tunnel approaches. On your left is Thomas Telford's ★ **Conwy Suspension Bridge**, built in 1826 to replace the ferry and for many years the only vehicular crossing. It is now pedestrianised with its Toll House (Easter to November, daily 10am–5pm) restored in period style by the National Trust. Robert Stephenson's tubular railway bridge, opened 12 years later runs alongside carrying the main Euston to Holyhead line.

Enclosed by battlemented walls, Conwy is one of the best preserved medieval fortified towns in Europe and ★★★ **Conwy Castle** (daily 10am–4pm, 6.30pm Easter to October) dominates arrival from the east. The castle was

Conwy and its castle

*Plas Mawr and
Britain's Smallest House*

begun in 1283, contemporarily with those at Harlech and Caernarfon, under the aegis of Edward I's talented military architect, James of St George. Within five years the work was completed and the castle's eight limewashed, conical-roofed towers stood sentinel over the threshold to Eryri. Views from the ★ **North West Tower** are especially fine but allow time to explore the complex and to absorb its fascinating history in the adjacent Visitor Centre.

Over a mile (1.7km) in total length, with five gateways and 21 towers, ★★ **Conwy Town Walls** have survived almost unscathed. Walking along the ramparts reveals bird's-eye views over 19th-century River Quay and the little town which boasts more than 200 buildings of special architectural interest. Notable among them are Elizabethan ★★ **Plas Mawr**, the recently restored headquarters of the Royal Cambrian Academy of Art; ★ **Aberconwy House**, the town's only surviving medieval merchant's house; and, down on the quayside, Britain's reputedly **Smallest House**.

Take the B5106 Trefriw road from the castle and follow it south along the pastoral ★ **Vale of Conwy**. A mile past Ty'n-y-groes, poorly signed on the left, is a driveway to Caerhun, lowest fording point on the River Conwy since Roman times. It was guarded then by a fort – Canovium – in whose northeast quadrant sits the tiny medieval **Church of St Mary**. The site is also accessible by footpath from Tal-y-cafn bridge just over a mile to the north. At Caerhun the Roman road from Chester struck westwards over wild hills to Abergwyngregyn and on to Caernarfon. Its bold line, too exposed for motor traffic, climbs as a rough track from the end of unclassified lanes above Rowen and Llanbedr-y-cennin to Bwlch y Ddeufaen at over 1,300ft (400m) and remains in use to this day by walkers and mountain bikers.

To the north of **Dolgarrog**, with its large aluminium works, the B5106 passes along a broad reach of undulating farmland before the Vale of Conwy narrows to a flat flood plain at **Trefriw**. En route stands **Trefriw Wells Spa** (Easter to October, daily 10am–5.30pm; November to Easter closed Sunday mornings), believed to have been discovered by soldiers of the XXth Roman Legion. The Victorians, with a penchant for 'taking the waters', added a Pump Room and Bath House to the original ancient grotto. Today's tour includes sampling the chalybeate spring. Trefriw itself clings to steep wooded hillside above

Llyn Crafnant

which lie two lakes, ★ **Crafnant** and **Geirionydd** (both have encircling footpaths). Their waters flow down the Afon Crafnant to ★ **Trefriw Woollen Mill** (shop, tearoom and turbine house open daily except Sundays, 10am–5pm; weaving in operation weekdays plus summer weekends), whose turbines power the 1950s vintage mill machinery. All processes can be followed, including the weaving of traditional Welsh tapestries and tweeds.

Tortuous lanes to the west penetrate ★★ **Gwydir Forest Park**, a fascinating region of mine-scarred hills and secretive lakes. There are forest trails, picnic and car parking areas. Where the B5106 swings left, take the right fork for Betws-y-Coed. The market town of **Llanrwst** lies just across the River Conwy spanned by the graceful, 17th-century three-arched **Pont Fawr**. Off the first bend on the B5106 stands **Gwydir Castle**, a Tudor mansion painstakingly restored following a fire in the 1920s. Just before joining the A5 at Betws-y-Coed the road crosses ★ **Pont-y-pair** ('Bridge of the Cauldron') from which intrepid youngsters plunge on hot summer days.

Pont Fawr in Llanrwst

Situated at the eastern gateway to Snowdonia National Park, **Betws-y-Coed** ('Chapel in the Wood') is built around the confluence of three rivers, the Conwy, the Llugwy and the Lledr. Popular with Victorian honeymooners, the village was put firmly on the map by the Birmingham watercolourist, David Cox. Over the years the main street of greystone cottages and hotels has sprouted a rash of craft shops, outdoor equipment stores and eating places to cater for increasingly broad tastes. Among the trippers mingle *bona fide* walkers, climbers, anglers and canoeists. Several easy walks start here, particularly up to **Llyn Elsi** by the Jubilee Path, to forest-fringed **Llyn y Parc**, and along the River Llugwy to the **Miners Bridge** – all waymarked.

Brave swimmers at Betws-y-Coed

17

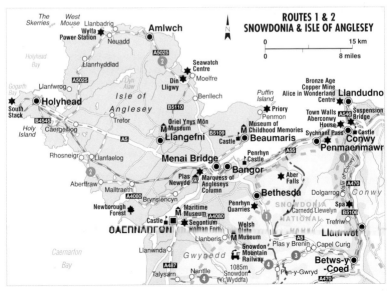

ROUTES 1 & 2
SNOWDONIA & ISLE OF ANGLESEY

0   15 km
0   8 miles

Gruffydd ap Dafydd

Betws has a station on the single track ★ **Conwy Valley Line** running from Llandudno Junction to Blaenau Ffestiniog *(see Route 3, page 28)* through stunning scenery. Behind the station, ignored by the crowds, sleeps the 14th-century **Old Church of St Michael & All Angels** containing an effigy of Gruffydd ap Dafydd, great nephew of Llywelyn the Last who fought in the wars of Edward III and the Black Prince. If it's closed, the key to the church can be obtained from the central complex known as **Royal Oak Stables** (daily 10am–6pm), which houses National Park and RSPB information centres dealing with all aspects of the area, from its wildlife and forestry to outdoor pursuits, history and topography.

The Swallow Falls

From Betws-y-Coed the A5 climbs slowly to ★ **Swallow Falls**, a beauty spot visited since the early 19th century where the Afon Llugwy drops 30ft (9m) into a deep pool, continuing as a single foaming torrent. In George Borrow's day, visitors were led down to the falls by a guide upon payment of a few pence; today the turnstile fee is still a modest one. Less than a mile ahead motorists pass **Ty Hyll** ('**The Ugly House**') which dates from the Middle Ages and is now the headquarters of the Snowdonia National Park Society (May to September, daily 9.30am–5pm).

As **Capel Curig** is approached there are majestic views first of Moel Siabod (2,861ft/872m) on the left, then to the Snowdon massif and the humpback Carneddau mountains. Capel Curig's equipment shops and friendly café serve the needs of the year-round outdoor fraternity, as does **Plas y Brenin**, Wales's National Centre for Mountain Activities, which runs courses in more than 50 disciplines.

Five miles (8km) ahead beside Thomas Telford's London to Holyhead highway, pinched between the frowning Glyder and Carneddau peaks, lies ★ **Llyn Ogwen**. Here, it is claimed, Sir Bedivere, last of Arthur's knights, cast Excalibur into the water. Llyn Ogwen is Snowdonia's shallowest lake with a mean depth of only 6ft (1.8m). Walk along the north shore fishermen's path to appreciate the rearing bulk of **Tryfan** (3,002ft/915m); its proximity to the A5 and its rocky ridges leading to twin summit boulders christened *Adam and Eve* attract large numbers of walkers. A path leading south from Ogwen Cottage to ★★ **Cwm Idwal** follows a rugged 2-mile (3-km) nature trail revealing in graphic form the region's fascinating glacial origins. From the far end of Llyn Idwal an exhilarating but very steep path climbs through the rocky cleft known as the **Devil's Kitchen** (**Twll Du**) to Llyn Cwn and on up to the boulder-strewn **Glyder** tops or the smoother-contoured Y Garn. On the lake's eastern side rise the **Idwal Slabs**, easy-angled rock faces often used by novice climbers 'learning the ropes'.

In the Devil's Kitchen

Wriggling from the mountains' grasp, the A5 delivers motorists down the dramatic **Nant Ffrancon Valley** to **Bethesda**, named after one of the town's many slate workers' chapels. It might as readily have been 'Jerusalem' or 'Siloam'. Southwest of the town, hemming it in, are the vast Penrhyn Slate Quarries that once employed 2,000 men and are reckoned to be the deepest in the world. Begun in Elizabethan times, they were greatly expanded at the initiative of Thomas Pennant from Liverpool, who married the Penrhyn estate heiress and himself became Baron Penrhyn in 1783. A short drive beyond the A55 towards Bangor will locate the National Trust's ★★ **Penrhyn Castle** (April to October, daily except Tuesdays 11am–5pm), Pennant's ostentatious, neo-Norman seat, set amidst glorious and extensive grounds. As well as fine interior craftsmanship there's an **Industrial Railway Museum**.

Turn right onto the A55 coastal Expressway to **Abergwyngregyn** which flanks the Carneddau foothills with wonderful views over to Anglesey and Conwy Bay. Note that a lane southeast from Abergwyngregyn leads to a Forest Enterprise car park near Bont Newydd, start of a popular and easy 3-mile (5-km) round walk to view ★ **Aber Falls**. The larger cascade – Rhaedr Fawr – plunges 170ft (52m) into the boulder-choked Afon Aber.

On the A55 beyond Llanfairfechan watch carefully for the turn-off to **Penmaenmawr**, much loved by the redoubtable Mr Gladstone but today a seaside town that has seen rather better days. Its *raison d'être* is the towering stone quarries behind on Penmaen Mawr ('Big Stone Headland'). From Penmaenmawr, take the unclassified road towards Dwygyfylchi and so to the craggy ★ **Sychnant Pass** on the old coaching route between Conwy and Bangor which avoided Penmaen Bach headland. There are walks in both directions from the pass, with marvellous views of Puffin Island and the Vale of Conwy.

Penrhyn Castle

Gathered for shearing in the Nant Ffrancon Valley

19

The Aber Falls

Marine theme at the Llys
Llywelyn Centre

Route 2

Anglesey (Ynys Môn)

Gogarth Bay

Llanfairpwllgwyngyll – Newborough – Holy Island – Amlwch – Moelfre – Llangefni – Beaumaris (93 miles/150km) *See map on page 17*

Anglesey – Ynys Môn to the Welsh – is Britain's largest offshore island. It is joined to the mainland by two engineering marvels which span the treacherous Menai Strait: Thomas Telford's elegant suspension bridge and George Stephenson's Britannia Bridge. Before they were built, visitors risked often hazardous ferry crossings at the mercy of tide and weather.

Heathland, pasture and fen spread gently westwards, punctuated by wind-honed copses and villages of single-storey, pebble-dashed houses crouched against the winter winds that sweep up through St George's Channel. The island's unique character distinguishes it from the rest of Snowdonia yet one is constantly reminded of its proximity by the viewcard panorama of mountains spread along the eastern horizon. Much of Anglesey's shoreline enjoys Heritage Coast or AONB status, a wonderful succession of dunes and river estuaries, islands, coves and bird-haunted sea cliffs; there are glorious sandy bays too.

Anglesey's long history has woven a rich tapestry of fascinating sites, from Neolithic times through the Industrial Revolution to the 20th century. In the fishing villages and around the coast, there are many associations with shipwreck and smuggling, while inland a profusion of wildlife co-exists with a rural economy that until the 19th century derived much of its power from windmills, the stumps of which still dot the countryside.

Windmills dot the countryside

The A4080 and A5025 roads all but encircle the island, with the A5 striking more directly northwest to its terminus at Holyhead. However, more intimate glimpses of coast and interior are gained by exploring country lanes along the way. A visit to Oriel Ynys Môn on the outskirts of Llangefni (*see page 24*) equips the visitor with many insights into the island's culture, history and environment.

From Bangor follow the A5122 and join the A5 over Stephenson's **Britannia Bridge** (Pont Britannia), built in 1850 to carry two railway tracks, each enclosed in an iron tube similar to the construction of the railway bridge over the River Conwy. A fire in 1970 so damaged the tubes that the bridge was closed while new arches were installed and a new road deck added on top.

Turn left onto the A4080 and note on the right the 100-ft (30m) **Marquess of Anglesey's Column**. It commemorates the Marquess's heroic wounding at the Battle of Waterloo, when he exclaimed to the Duke of Wellington: 'By god sir, I've lost my leg!', to which the Duke replied: 'By god, so you have!'

Watch for the A4080's left turn at **Llanfairpwllgwyngyllgogerychwyrndrobwllllantysiliogogogoch** ('St Mary's Church in the hollow of the white hazel near the rapid whirlpool of St Tysilio close to the red cave'). This tongue-twisting place name was probably a 19th-century hoax to attract tourists; certainly it is Britain's longest, with a railway station nameplate of national repute.

Llanfairpwllgwyn... station **21**

In 1½ miles (2.5km) the road passes the National Trust's ★★ **Plas Newydd** (Easter to end-September daily except Saturdays; October Fridays and Sundays only. House noon–5pm, Gardens 11am–5.30pm). This magnificent early 19th-century Gothic and neoclassical mansion is set in sloping parkland overlooking the Menai Strait and the Snowdonia mountains. Its interior *pièce de résistance* is an extraordinary 58-ft (18-m) long *trompe l'oeil* mural painted in 1937 by Rex Whistler.

Woodland at Plas Newydd

Brysiencyn stands surrounded by an ancient landscape of prehistoric dolmens and burial mounds. Reached via by-roads is ★ **Anglesey Sea Zoo** (daily 10am–6pm), the focal point of which is a large aquarium. The A4080 continues to Newborough at the island's southwest tip. Since Elizabeth I's reign marram grass has been planted to stabilise the shifting dunes here in ★ **Newborough Warren**. Before 1930, when afforestation began, the grass was woven into mats and brushes while the warren's rabbit population provided valuable protein for the local diet. A forestry toll road runs down to ★ **Llanddwyn Bay's** 1 mile (6.5km) long beach and there are walks in the 2,000-acre (800-hectare) Newborough Forest. The area has been designated a National Nature Reserve.

Llys Llywelyn sculpture

For almost 30 years before his death in 1979 the wildlife artist Charles Tunnicliffe lived at **Malltraeth**, recording the island's landscapes and especially its birds. His work is represented in Oriel Ynys Môn at Llangefni.

Immense sandhills separate **Aberffraw's** beach from road and village. Here was an ancient seat of the powerful Princes of Gwynedd and their main Court (Llys) up to the 13th century. Nothing remains of the original timber buildings but this important site and the neighbouring coastal heritage is explained in detail at the **Llys Llywelyn Centre** (Easter to September, daily except Mondays 11am–5pm), with guided walks during the summer.

Rhosneigr (from Rhos-y-Neidr, 'Moor of the Adder') sits on a little rocky promontory at the mouth of the Afon Crigyll, its demure whitewashed cottages belying a darker past when a gang of wreckers lured ships onto this rugged shore. They were finally caught and hanged at Beaumaris in 1741, later to become the subject of a local ballad.

Fork left 500m northeast of Llanfaelog, joining the A5 at Bryngwran for Holyhead. At Caergeiliog plane-spotters can take the lane south to the railway bridge at Llanfairyneubwll, or further to Carnau, there to watch the comings and goings at **RAF Valley** with its training school for jet pilots and air-sea rescue station.

South Stack and excursion party

A detour out to ★ **Holy Island (Ynys Gybi)** is recommended. The B4545 to Treaddur Bay gives way to tortuous lanes over to ★ **South Stack**, a rocky islet reached by pedestrian bridge at the bottom of 350 steps. Over 4,000 pairs of seabirds breed in this RSPB reserve each spring and early summer, observable from the ★ **Ellin's Tower Centre** (Easter to September, daily 11am–5pm). The nearby **Gogarth Bay** sea cliffs are a popular rock-climbing venue and there are clifftop walks to North Stack. At 722ft (220m), **Holyhead Mountain** is Anglesey's highest ground by far, with views to match. Hut circles and the large Caer-y-Twr hillfort indicate mankind's occupation of this exposed peninsula over many centuries.

Holyhead (Caergybi) is Anglesey's largest town and an important seaport for services to Dublin and Dun Laoghaire. The arrival of Telford's road from London in 1821, marked by a triumphal Doric arch, and the railway shortly afterwards, transformed the harbour's fortunes. A huge breakwater almost 2 miles (3km) long was built (it took 30 years) to protect the anchorage's 700 acres (280 hectares) from northwesterly gales.

Lanes branch out from the A5025 towards the shore of Holyhead Bay where coves and low cliffs alternate towards Carmel Head. Offshore lie **The Skerries** and **West Mouse** islands, hazards in the days of sail when anxious Liverpool shipowners awaited news of their vessels.

Anglesey's north coast is closely shadowed by roads, but there is a fine stretch of coastal footpath too, especially between Cemaes and Amlwch. Car parks at both ends of **Cemlyn Bay**'s great shingle bank and lagoon allow access to view seabirds or walk. The **Magnox Wylfa Power Station** may be visited (daily 9.30am– 4.30pm; hourly guided tours) and a Nature Trail followed.

Before Amlwch's ascendancy in the late-18th century, **Cemaes** and **Porthlechog** were centres for fishing, coastal trade and smuggling. **Amlwch** itself became a boom town when top-grade copper ore was discovered in nearby Parys Mountain during 1768. The ore was dug in open-cast workings and within 30 years the population had exploded to 6,000. Competition from cheaper American and African copper eventually ended the UK boom. The 'moonscape' of **Parys Mountain**, along with **Llyn Alaw**, Anglesey's largest lake, lie just to the south.

Extensive sands characterise Anglesey's sheltered eastern coast, particularly bordering Dulas, Lligwy and Red Wharf bays; in between, however, treacherous rocks have caused many a shipwreck. It was north of ★ **Moelfre** in October 1859 that the steam clipper *Royal Charter*, inward bound from the Australian goldfields, foundered in huge seas with the loss of 450 lives and an estimated £370,000 of prospectors' gold. Visit Moelfre's **Seawatch Centre** (Easter to September, daily except Mondays 10am–5pm) for all things maritime. The native Celtic settlement of ★ **Din Lligwy** lies just to the west, in a clearing in the woodland beyond the ruins of the eponymous chapel. Dating from around AD400, it is one of the most impressive ancient sites in Britain, surviving as a place where ordinary people lived; some buildings still possess substantial walls with doorposts and traces of drainage systems across

Picturesque Moelfre

23

Cemaes harbour

Oriel Ynys Mon

the floor. For unrivalled panoramic views, climb to the little 584-ft (178-m) summit of ★ **Mynydd Bodafon** reached up a lane off the A5025.

Half a mile south of the Moelfre roundabout, turn right onto the B5110. The administrative capital of Anglesey and its principal market town, **Llangefni** epitomises the island's rural Welsh heart. Although the traditional cattle market has moved out of the town centre, The Square, near the Bull Hotel, remains a constantly bustling focal point. On the town's outskirts along the B5111 to the north stands ★★ **Oriel Ynys Môn** (Tuesday to Sunday and Bank Holiday Mondays 10.30am–5pm), which houses an excellent permanent exhibition featuring Anglesey's history, culture and environment, as well as shows of artists' work.

Beaumaris Castle

Follow the B5109 via Pentraeth to **Beaumaris** (from *beau maris*, Norman-French for 'beautiful marsh'). Last in Edward I's chain of coastal fortresses against the Welsh, ★★ **Beaumaris Castle** (daily 9.30am–6.30pm; 4pm winter closing) is also Britain's most technically perfect medieval castle, with concentric rings of defensive walls inside a deep moat; a jetty enabled provisioning to take place from the sea.

Opposite stands the 17th-century ★ **Courthouse** (daily during Easter, May weekends and Whitsun to end-September), while behind the Parish Church to the west will be found the ★ **Gaol** (open as Courthouse). Both provide grim reminders of justice and prison life in earlier times.

Museum of Childhood Memories

Also opposite the Castle, nine themed rooms crammed with toys, artefacts and memorabilia from 150 years of British family life are presented by the ★ **Museum of Childhood Memories** (Easter to November 1st, daily 10.30am–5.30pm; Sundays 12–5pm).

To visit ★ **Penmon Priory** ruins and **St Seiriol's Well**, take the B5109 north and follow signs along the narrow access lanes. The original priory, founded here and on neighbouring Priestholm (Puffin Island) in the 6th century by the hermit St Seiriol, was burned down by the Danes. The present ★ **Penmon Church**, containing some splendid Norman features, dates from the 12th century, the associated monastic buildings from the 13th to the 16th centuries. East of the priory, a massive dovecote was built around 1600 to house up to 1,000 pigeons destined for the table of local landowner Sir Richard Bulkeley.

The Menai Suspension Bridge

The A545 leads along the wooded shoreline of the Menai Strait to Menai Bridge where Thomas Telford's ★★ **Suspension Bridge** is crossed. Having overcome the greatest challenge on his London to Holyhead turnpike, Telford himself drove home the final suspension chain link on the world's first large-scale iron bridge of this design, which opened in 1826.

Route 3

Snowdon seen across the waters of Llynau Mymbyr

The Moelwyn Hills and Porthmadog

Betws-y-Coed – Capel Curig – Beddgelert – Porthmadog – Blaenau Ffestiniog – Dolwyddelan – Betws-y-Coed (81 miles/130km) *See map on pages 30–1*

Throughout Snowdonia one finds echoes of those intrepid Victorians who, marooned at home by the Napoleonic wars in Europe, made resorts out of sleepy hamlets and, influenced by contemporary Romanticism, set the trend for enjoying the great outdoors. Angling, walking, climbing, sketching or simply admiring the scenery all drew visitors to this part of Wales, among them William Wordsworth, Sir Walter Scott and the painter William Turner. This popularisation spurred the development of such places as Betws-y-Coed, Capel Curig, Beddgelert and Dolwyddelan.

Porthmadog then and now

The less well-off local population still had to work for a living, often in arduous conditions. Copper mining, agriculture and fishing continued to employ labour as they had for centuries but it was the building trade's insatiable appetite for roofing slate that brought about the greatest changes and opportunities. The hills around Blaenau Ffestiniog and many other locations were devastated by quarrying, their slate transported by narrow-gauge railway to quaysides on the coast, such as those at Porthmadog.

From **Betws-y-Coed** the A5 climbs past **Swallow Falls** to reach the straggling village of **Capel Curig** *(see Route 1, page 18)*. Take the A4086 past **Plas y Brenin**, Wales's National Centre for Mountain Activities, which runs courses in more than 50 disciplines, and enjoy a ★★ **classic view of Snowdon** seen across the waters of Llynau Mym-

byr. The Nantygwryd valley forms a broad trench between Moel Siabod (2,861ft/872m), and the Glyder range whose rugged slopes fill northern views right along to the **Pen-y-Gwryd** junction. Up to the right lies Pen-y-Pass, starting point for two popular paths up Snowdon and, beyond, the Llanberis Pass (*see Route 4, page 35*).

Keep straight on along the A498 and in a mile or so there are lay-bys from which to admire the Snowdon massif from the east. Cwm Dyli, a deep U-shaped hollow containing hydro-electric pipelines, was scoured out by an Ice Age glacier which then turned abruptly southwest to form Nant Gwynant. The road coils narrowly downhill to beautiful, shingle-beached ★ **Llyn Gwynant**. At its southern end hills encroach forming a glen connecting with **Llyn Dinas**. Strangely reminiscent of a Chinese landscape painting, this area was chosen in 1958 as a location for filming *Inn of the Sixth Happiness*. Unseen up to the left, the Moelwyn hills cradle myriad small lakes, but they are quite remote and only accessible on foot.

Llyn Gwynant

Yr Aran (2,451ft/747m), rears a shapely head to the north and the road reaches ★★ **Sygun Copper Mine** (Easter to September, daily 10am–5pm; October to Easter, daily 10.30am–4pm). Begun around 1830 but never a commercial success owing to the low-grade ore, Sygun mine was abandoned in 1903. Extensively restored since then, it provides fascinating tours of the tunnels, chambers, ore veins and mining processes.

Exploring the Sygun Copper Mine

There are scenic paths over to Cwm Bychan and the Pass of Aberglaslyn, while an unclassified mountain road with picnic areas runs from Pont Bethania through Nantmor. However the main road itself goes through ★ **Beddgelert**, clustered prettily around the confluence of the Glaslyn and Colwyn rivers beneath the dominant presence of Moel Hebog (2,566ft/782m). Alfred Bestall, who created the comic character Rupert Bear, was born here; he died in 1986. Although more probably derived from Celert, a 6th-century Celtic saint, Beddgelert has been immortalised by the apocryphal legend of Gelert, Llywelyn the Great's faithful hound. **Gelert's Grave** can be seen just to the south of the village; by following the south-flowing Afon Glaslyn beyond it, continuing along the trackbed of the old **Welsh Highland Railway**, it is possible to walk to the car park at Nantmor near the pine-clad **Pass of Aberglaslyn**, a distance of about 1½ miles (2.5km). The narrow-gauge railway was intended to link Porthmadog with Caernarfon but customer demand failed to meet expectations and the line closed in 1937. A short section from Porthmadog has been revived for steam pleasure trips.

Beddgelert and Gelert's Grave

Having left Beddgelert, keep right at the Pass of Aberglaslyn, still on the A498. First through woods with tantalising views of Tremadog Bay, then clinging to the western edge of reclaimed marshland on the Afon Glaslyn's flood plain, the road reaches **Tremadog**, best known for its roadside rock-climbing crags and the handy Eric's Café. T.E. Lawrence (Lawrence of Arabia) was born in the village which was developed as a staging post in the early 1800s by William Madocks, Member of Parliament for Boston, Lincolnshire. It formed part of his ambitious, though ultimately unsuccessful, scheme to establish a new mail route to Ireland using Porth Dinllaen on the north coast of the Lleyn Peninsula *(see Route 5, page 40)*.

Turn left onto the A487. These days **Porthmadog** is a bustling holiday centre for outdoor activities of all kinds but in times past its prosperity was dependent on the slate industry. From its quaysides, ships loaded with Ffestiniog slate, brought down by narrow-gauge railway from the great quarries around Blaenau Ffestiniog, set sail for destinations worldwide. The town, whose grid plan was designed by Madocks, has a **Maritime Museum** (Whitsun to end-September, daily 10am–6pm), housed in a surviving slate shed on one of the harbour wharves and recalling its past as an industrial port. A path from the harbour leads along to neighbouring Borth-y-Gest, another erstwhile slate port with a curving quay backed by cottages.

Ffestiniog Railway

From the necessity of shipping slate out grew the world-renowned, narrow-gauge ★★★ **Ffestiniog Railway** (daily throughout the high season but consult timetable). It began life in 1836, conveying industrial slate from the great Ffestiniog quarries to Porthmadog quay. Since 1954, when the line was enthusiastically rescued from oblivion, it has enjoyed burgeoning popularity. The full 13½-mile (22-km) journey takes an hour each way and provides spectacular views from the carriage windows, especially outside the season of full tree foliage. Connections with the ★ **Conwy Valley Line** at Blaenau Ffestiniog open up numerous travel permutations. More details on the railway can be found at the small **Ffestiniog Railway Museum** (daily 10am–5.30pm) at Porthmadog station. Just to the north of Porthmadog there is more narrow-gauge railway interest at the ★ **Welsh Highland Railway Centre** (daily Easter to October but consult timetable), complete with a short stretch of operational line.

Cnicht from The Cob

Cheek by jowl with the railway, the road crosses the mile-long embankment across the Glaslyn estuary known as ★ **The Cob** (small toll), a famous Madocks creation behind which some 7,000 acres (2,800 hectares) were reclaimed from the sea. If visibility is clear there are stunning mountain views over the estuary. The shapeliest cone is **Cnicht** (2,261ft/689m), the so-called 'Welsh Matterhorn'. In about a mile, **Minffordd** is reached where the Ffestiniog

27

Market day in Blaenau Ffestiniog

Llechwedd Slate Caverns

Blaenau Ffestiniog: a town built on slate

and main Cambrian Coast line between Pwllheli and Aberystwyth intersect, each with a station allowing interchange. Beyond **Penrhyndeudraeth** (headquarters of the Snowdonia National Park) the A487 follows the Afon Dwyryd to **Tan-y-Bwlch** in the lovely Vale of Ffestiniog. Once over the river it joins the A496 near the pretty village of **Maentwrog**, named after a large stone in the churchyard said to have been thrown there from the hills above by the giant Twrog. The novelist Thomas Love Peacock spent much time here, eventually marrying the local rector's daughter. Another literary association involves the great English poet Gerard Manley Hopkins who found inspiration for his work during a visit here.

When the National Park was designated in 1952, **Blaenau Ffestiniog** and neighbouring Tanygrisiau were excluded: national park criteria were hardly met, it was argued, by an area of decaying slate tips, disused quarries and high local unemployment requiring an influx of alternative industries. It still rains for over 100 days each year in Blaenau Ffestiniog and by traditional yardsticks the surroundings remain bleak, yet perversely this has become part of Blaenau's very appeal. Since those early days public perceptions have changed, particularly in regard to industrial archaeology which, as it happens, has transformed Blaenau's fortunes. Witness, for example, the success of the ★★ **Llechwedd Slate Caverns** (daily 10am–5.15pm, 4.15pm in winter) and **Gloddfa Ganol Slate Mine** (Easter to October, weekdays 10am–5.30pm and high season Sundays), both highly educational tourist attractions. At Llechwedd, there are two tours available: a guided tour half a mile into the side of the mountain by tram; and a deep mine tour on Britain's deepest underground railway. It is fascinating to note that because they

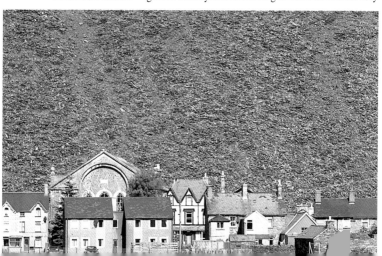

only worked by candlelight, the miners never actually saw the huge caverns they created.

The pumped-storage **Ffestiniog Power Station** stands just to the southwest with a Visitor Centre and guided tours (10am–4.30pm daily Easter week and mid-July to mid-August; otherwise closed weekends). At Tanygrisiau there are walks from the road-end up to **Llyn Cwmorthin** in a valley strewn with evocative relics from a bygone era of intensive slate working. A derelict chapel, ruined workers' cottages and abandoned slate sheds crouch beneath the brooding Moelwyn hills whose highest point – Moelwyn Mawr (2,526ft/770m) – overlooks the Stwlan Dam.

Relics of the past at Llyn Cwmorthin

The A470 climbs determinedly north to the **Crimea Pass** at 1,263ft (385m) above sea level. It was not named after the mid 19th-century war but after a pub that once stood on the site of the present car park at the top. After locals repeatedly complained of rowdiness in 1910 it was demolished with true non-conformist vindictiveness.

Coming down off the pass facing vast views ahead, the road descends as a long dramatic sweep into the wooded valley of the Afon Lledr. It crosses the railway line, which has not long since emerged from a 2-mile (3.5km) long tunnel, to reach ★ **Dolwyddelan Castle** (daily all year – tickets from entrance or adjacent farmhouse). Situated on a knoll on the southern slopes of Moel Siabod, a little way from the roadside car park along a good path, the castle stands over the route from the Conwy and Lledr valleys over to Dyffryn Maentwrog – broadly the way just followed. It was built by the Welsh in the late 12th century, but its upper parts are a 19th-century reconstruction. Tradition has it that Llywelyn the Great was born here. The castle was besieged and fell to the invading English in January 1283, though subsequently in the late 15th century it was reoccupied by Maredudd ab Ieuan, a descendant of the Prince of Powys who led Welsh resistance against Henry I in the 12th century. In **Dolwyddelan** village, south of the main road, stands the delightful little 16th-century ★ **Old Church**.

29

Dolwyddelan Castle

With numerous twists and turns the A470 drops eastwards towards the confluence of the Lledr and Machno rivers in woodland that becomes outstandingly beautiful in autumn colours. Up to the south, but only accessible on very narrow lanes, will be found the National Trust's ★ **Ty Mawr** (Easter to end-September, Thursday to Sunday 12–5pm; October Thursday, Friday and Sunday 12–4pm), birthplace of William Morgan who first translated the Bible into Welsh. Further south still, **Penmachno** village is well known for its weaving tradition and ★ **Woollen Mill** (daily 10am–5.30pm). A minor road to the west of the river makes for a more pleasant entry to Betws-y-Coed.

Riding stables near Ty Mawr

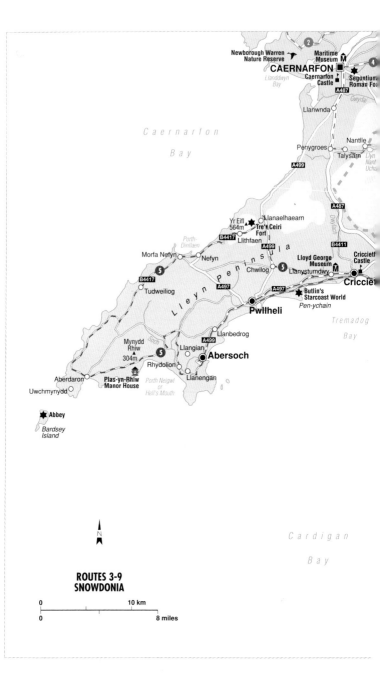

ROUTES 3-9
SNOWDONIA

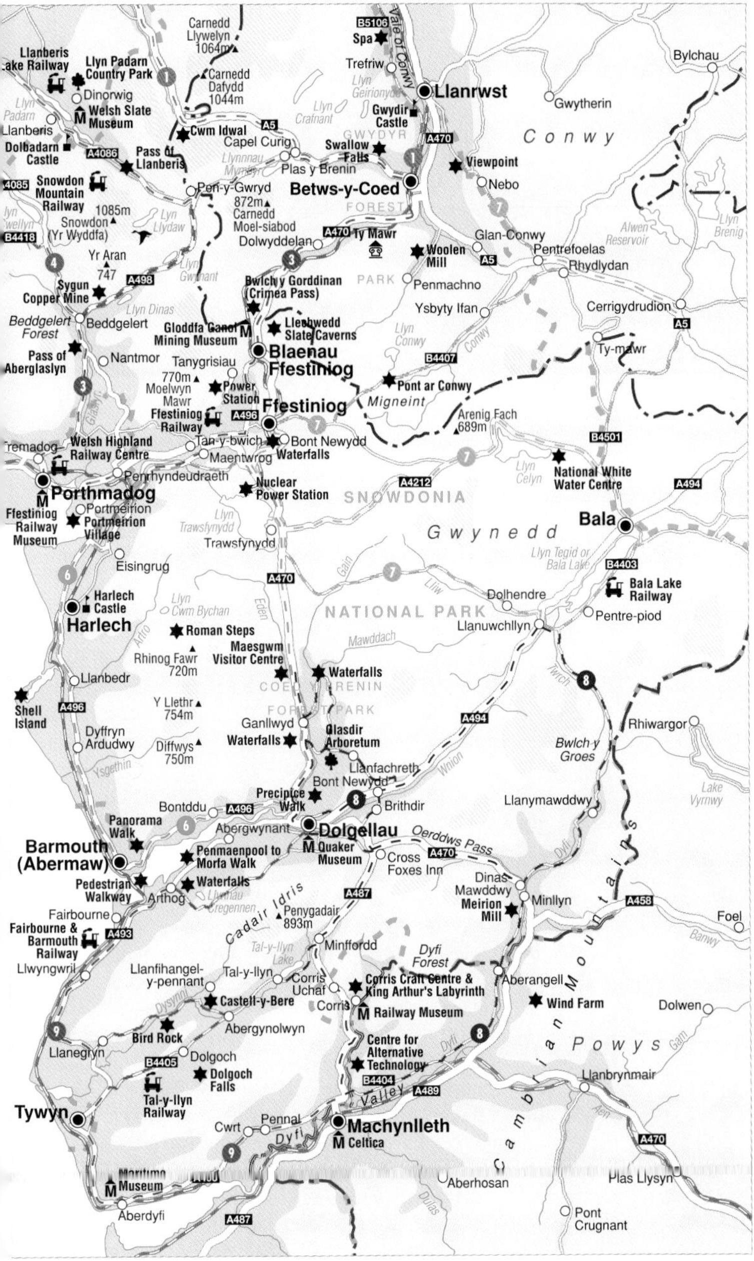

Carnedd Llywelyn 1064m
Llanberis Lake Railway
Llyn Padarn Country Park
Dinorwig
Llyn Padarn
Welsh Slate Museum
Llanberis
Dolbadarn Castle
A4086
Pass of Llanberis
Carnedd Dafydd 1044m
Cwm Idwal
A5
Capel Curig
Llynnau Mymbyr
Plas y Brenin
B5106
Spa
Vale of Conwy
Trefriw
Llyn Geirionydd
Llanrwst
Llyn Crafnant
Gwydir Castle
GWYDYR
A470
Swallow Falls
Betws-y-Coed
FOREST
Viewpoint
Nebo
Bylchau
Gwytherin
Conwy
A4085
Snowdon Mountain Railway
1085m
Snowdon (Yr Wyddfa)
Llyn Llydaw
B4418
Pen-y-Gwryd
872m
Carnedd Moel-siabod
Dolwyddelan
Ty Mawr
Woolen Mill
Glan-Conwy
Pentrefoelas
Rhydlydan
Alwen Reservoir
Llyn Brenig
Yr Aran 747
A498
Sygun Copper Mine
Llyn Gwynant
Bwlch y Gorddinan (Crimea Pass)
PARK
Penmachno
Ysbyty Ifan
Cerrigydrudion
Llyn Dinas
Beddgelert Forest
Beddgelert
Gloddfa Ganol Mining Museum
Llechwedd Slate Caverns
Blaenau Ffestiniog
Llyn Conwy
B4407
Ty-mawr
Pass of Aberglaslyn
Nantmor
Tanygrisiau
770m Moelwyn Mawr
Power Station
Pont ar Conwy
Migneint
Arenig Fach 689m
Ffestiniog Railway
A496
Ffestiniog
Tremadog
Welsh Highland Railway Centre
Tan-y-bwlch
Maentwrog
Bont Newydd
Waterfalls
B4501
Llyn Celyn
National White Water Centre
A4212
A494
Porthmadog
Penrhyndeudraeth
Nuclear Power Station
SNOWDONIA
Ffestiniog Railway Museum
Portmeirion
Portmeirion Village
Llyn Trawsfynydd
Trawsfynydd
Gwynedd
Bala
Llyn Tegid or Bala Lake
B4403
Eisingrug
A470
Bala Lake Railway
Harlech Castle
Harlech
Llyn Cwm Bychan
Eden
NATIONAL PARK
Dolhendre
Pentre-piod
Llanuwchllyn
Roman Steps
Rhinog Fawr 720m
Maesgwm Visitor Centre
Mawddach
Waterfalls
COED Y BRENIN
FOREST PARK
Llanbedr
Shell Island
A496
Y Llethr 754m
Ganllwyd
A494
Rhiwargor
Dyffryn Ardudwy
Waterfalls
Glasdir Arboretum
Bwlch y Groes
Diffwys 750m
Llanfachreth
Wnion
Ysgethin
Bont Newydd
Lake Vyrnwy
Bontddu
Precipice Walk
Brithdir
Llanymawddwy
Panorama Walk
Abergwynant
Dolgellau
Oerddws Pass
Quaker Museum
Barmouth (Abermaw)
Penmaenpool to Morfa Walk
Cross Foxes Inn
A470
Pedestrian Walkway
Waterfalls
Arthog
Llynau Cregennen
A487
Dinas Mawddwy
Minllyn
Meirion Mill
A458
Fairbourne
Cadair Idris
Penygadair 893m
Foel
Fairbourne & Barmouth Railway
A493
Tal-y-llyn Lake
Minffordd
Dyfi Forest
Banwy
Llwyngwril
Llanfihangel-y-pennant
Tal-y-llyn
Corris Uchaf
Corris Craft Centre & King Arthur's Labyrinth
Aberangell
Wind Farm
Castell-y-Bere
Corris
Railway Museum
Dolwen
Abergynolwyn
Bird Rock
Centre for Alternative Technology
Powys
Llanegryn
B4405
Dolgoch
Dolgoch Falls
B4404
Llanbrynmair
Tal-y-llyn Railway
Valley
A489
Tywyn
Pennal
Machynlleth
Celtica
Cwrt
Dyfi
Cambrian Mountains
A470
Maritime Museum
Aberhosan
Plas Llysyn
Aberdyfi
A487
Dulas
Pont Crugnant

Route planning at Pen-y-Pass

Route 4

The Llanberis Pass and Snowdon from Caernarfon

Caernarfon – Llanberis – Pen-y-Pass – Beddgelert Forest Park – Nantlle – Penygroes – Caenarfon (38 miles/62km) *See map on page 30–1*

No visit to Snowdonia is complete without seeing Yr Wyddfa (Snowdon's Welsh name) at close quarters. Rising to 3,560ft (1,085m) it is the highest peak in England and Wales and one that offers itself generously (some might say too generously) to all who seek to explore its great crags and cwms.

There are six main tracks to the summit, while the less mobile may scale the heights by means of the famous Snowdon Mountain Railway. Needless to say, inexperienced hillwalkers should climb up only in good weather and should wear appropriate clothing.

On the Miners' Track (above), and the Pig Track (below)

Yr Wyddfa means 'tomb' or 'monument', a reference to the burial of the legendary Rhita Gawr, an ogre with a predilection for slaying kings who was himself killed at the summit by King Arthur. Botanist Thomas Johnson wrote the first account of an ascent in 1639 but it was Thomas Pennant's published tours that popularised the mountain in the late 18th century and another Thomas – Telford – whose London to Holyhead road provided the accessibility. By the 1830s guiding was already proving profitable, often using horses to convey visitors by the easier Llanberis Track. As early as 1854, on his famous tour of Wales, George Borrow found the track 'thronged with tourists as far as the eye could reach...' Accommodation and refreshments became available in wooden huts clustered around the huge summit cairn and operated by

competing hotels in the valley. When the first train service began in 1896, a new era of summit building was started, culminating in the demolition of the by-then squalid huts. In the 1930s, construction began of the present complex designed by Clough Williams-Ellis, creator of the Portmeirion Italianate village. It was extensively refurbished in 1983 to cope with ever-increasing visitor numbers.

Caernarfon and its castle

But first down to sea-level. **Caernarfon** is a busy holiday town, market and administrative centre. Its old streets and alleyways, its Georgian houses around **The Square** and its historic inns like the 'Black Boy' and 'Hole in the Wall', all exude flavours from a diverse past. So, too, does the **Segontium Roman Fort** (daily March to October, 9.30am–5.30pm; November to February closed one hour earlier) to the southeast of the town centre on the A4085, where the foundations of the fort garrisoned by the 20th Augustan legion can still be seen. The garrison stood guard over what came to be called Watling Street, a line of communication of great strategic importance.

But above all Caernarfon is synonymous with the magnificent ★★★ **Castle** (daily Easter to late-October 9.30am–6.30pm; late-October to Easter 9.30am–4pm). This was the largest of Edward I's network of fortifications, as if to underline his subjugation of the Welsh. Although begun, along with Conwy Castle, in 1283, it was to be 43 years before Edward's son, the first English Prince of Wales, completed the project. Twice unsuccessfully besieged by Owain Glyndwr, fought over during the Civil Wars and captured by Parliamentary forces in 1646, the castle was finally condemned for demolition in 1660. Happily the exterior walls and three towers remain intact and are hugely impressive, though most of the interior has been lawned. The present Prince of Wales was invested here on 1 July 1969. Queen's Tower houses the fascinating ★ **Regimental Museum** of the Royal Welsh Fusiliers.

The Seiont II

Much of the town's present countenance dates from the 19th century when it became a thriving slate port, and also well worth visiting is the **Maritime Museum** (daily Whitsun to end-September, 11am–3pm) based at Victoria Dock and including a 1937 steam dredger – *Seiont II* – moored on Slate Quay at the mouth of the Afon Seiont.

From Caernarfon, take the A4086 east to the shores of **Llyn Padarn** and **Llanberis**. The town's location at the foot of Snowdon and its plethora of visitor attractions ensure a brisk summer trade, though during the winter a rather more traditional Welsh character is revealed.

To the left of the A4086, on the south shore of Llyn Padarn, is the **Electric Mountain Centre** (Easter to end-September, daily 9.30am– 5.30pm; January to Easter

The Snowdon Mountain Railway

Dinorwig Slate Quarries

Expert at work in the Welsh Slate Museum

closed Monday to Wednesday), the base for bus tours leading for half a mile into the bowels of the ★★ **Dinorwig Pumped Storage Power Station**, the largest underground power station in Europe, commissioned in 1984. Visitors are shown the turbines and generators, and back at the centre there are audio-visual presentations and hands-on electricity exhibitions.

Near the eastern end of Llanberis is the ★★★ **Snowdon Mountain Railway** (daily, first train 9am, mid-March to end-October. Subject to weather and minimum demand). Whether ridden in or simply watched, the little trains make a stirring sight. Although beset with initial objections and technical difficulties, the rack-and-pinion track was laid in an astonishing 72 days during 1895–6. Since then increasing numbers of visitors have enjoyed the excursion – an hour each way with 30 minutes at the summit. The **Llanberis Track** up Snowdon, roughly parallel to the railway, begins from the road opposite the Royal Victoria Hotel.

The A4086 next approaches **Llyn Peris** and the vast hillside terraces of **Dinorwig Slate Quarries**. Covering 700 acres (280 hectares) and rising some 2,000ft (600m) up the flanks of Elidir Fawr, they were the largest of their kind in Britain during their heyday, employing over 3,000 men. The slate was taken to Port Dinorwig (Y Felinheli) on the Menai Strait by narrow-gauge railway, now partially revived as the passenger-carrying **Llanberis Lake Railway** (daily Easter to October 10am–4pm), set in Padarn Country Park with its numerous walking trails and boating on the lake. Beneath the slate quarries, in the original Dinorwig Quarry buildings, is the ★★ **Welsh Slate Museum** (daily Easter to end-September 9.30am–5.30pm; October to Easter weekdays 9.30am–4pm), where visitors can still see craftsmen cutting slate 'the old way' and are shown the gigantic waterwheel, the biggest in mainland Britain and, with a diameter of 54ft (17m), one of the biggest in the world.

The adjacent **Dolbadarn Castle** (daily all year), built on a grassy knoll to guard the overland route between Caernarfon and Conwy, today presides over a tract of Welsh landscape ravaged and re-shaped by civilisation: changed indeed from 1800 when the artist William Turner sketched and painted the 40ft (12m) round tower silhouetted against a lowering sky. The fortress holds a grim history. Owain ap Grufydd was imprisoned here for 22 years by his brother Llewelyn the Great who became the last independent Prince of Gwynedd. Llywelyn's grandson, Llywelyn the Last, made Dolbadarn his stronghold but was eventually forced to flee; he was captured and executed at Shrewsbury in 1283. With his death, Welsh resistance to Edward I's invasion finally came to an end.

Grey crags soaring above skirts of scree and boulders close in beyond Nant Peris. With innumerable classic routes on the precipices of Glyder Fawr to the north and Snowdon to the south, the ★★ **Llanberis Pass** has become a mecca for rock-climbers. Halfway up the pass on the left soars the great prow of Dinas Cromlech. Breakthroughs in the evolution of climbing took place here with Joe Brown's ascent of *Cenotaph Corner* in the 1950s, Pete Livesey's *Right Wall* and Ron Fawcett's *Fly on the Wall* in the 1970s. One of the most famous routes by Joe Brown and Don Whillans was *Cemetery Gates*. The road (built c.1830) is narrow and what few parking bays exist are usually occupied by climbers' vehicles. It is impossible not to be moved by the awesome scenery, even from a car, and many visitors are naturally tempted to park at ★ **Pen-y-Pass**, 1,168ft (356m). However, the car park there is notoriously over-subscribed (and expensive) so an alternative is to catch the bus up and back from Llanberis. The inn at the pass is now the Gorphwysfa youth hostel.

Behind the car park begin two popular paths to Snowdon summit. The **Miners' Track** was constructed in 1856 to serve the Britannia Copper Mine situated high under the mountain's east face. The **Pig Track** (after Bwlch y Moch – 'Pass of the Pigs' – which it crosses) is a more rugged approach. Both tracks converge higher up, ascending the zig-zags to join the Llanberis Track and railway for the final 300ft (90m) to the summit. The Miners' Track as far as Llyn Llydaw, even as far as Glaslyn, presents no difficulties and makes an enjoyable ramble. Both routes take about 3 hours up and about 2 hours back.

Cut into the steep face of Moel Berfedd and with dizzy views down Nant Gwynant, the road descends to the **Pen-y-Gwryd Hotel**. Pen-y-Gwryd translates as 'Head of Cai's Fathomwide Pass', from Cai, one of Arthur's knights who,

Llanberis Pass and climbers

legend has it, was massive enough to block the pass with his outstretched hands. The old inn here continues to accommodate hillgoers as well as passing tourists in a style appropriate to its unique situation and history. Not only did it once host the pioneers of early British rock-climbing but Everest expeditions based their training programmes here.

Turn right at the T-junction and follow the A498 towards Beddgelert, as described in Route 3 (*see page 26*). Between ★ **Llyn Gwynant** and **Llyn Dinas**, a small car park at Pont Bethania denotes the start of Snowdon's **Watkin Path**. Constructed by Sir Edward Watkin, a railway engineer and early protagonist of the Channel Tunnel, it was officially opened at a ceremony in 1892 by none other than the great statesman W.E. Gladstone. As the commemorative plaque further up the path records: 'The Multitude sang Cymric hymns and Land of my Fathers'.

Breakfast at Beddgelert Forest Park

From Beddgelert continue on the A4085 Caernarfon road. Foothills to the west are clothed in the pine and larch of **Beddgelert Forest Park**. Forest Enterprise has a large and well appointed campsite here as well as a number of waymarked trails. Further on lies Llyn-y-Gader, an anglers' lake mirroring the peaks along the Nantlle Ridge at its back. Almost opposite, to the east of the road, will be found a car park for Snowdon's **Rhy-Ddu Path**. In clear visibility almost the whole route to the summit can be seen from here.

Less than 2 miles (3km) further along the A4086 stands the Snowdon Ranger youth hostel set above the waters of ★ **Llyn Cwellyn**, home to the rare char, or red-bellied Alpine trout. It was here, on his journey through Wales in 1854, that George Borrow chatted with a local guide who offered to lead him up Snowdon and whose profession gave the **Snowdon Ranger Track** its name.

A less direct but more rewarding return to Caernarfon is made by turning west at **Rhy-Ddu** onto the B4418. Quite soon it passes **Llyn Dywarchen** and squeezes through **Drws-y-coed** ('The Wooded Pass') between the crags and scree of Craig y Bera and the menacing northern precipice of Y Garn to reach the ★ **Nantlle Valley** (Dyffryn Nantlle). Passing Llyn Nantlle Uchaf, the Talysarn slate quarries and terraces of miners' cottages, the A487 is reached at Penygroes with its trim chapels and memories of altogether busier times over a century ago.

To conclude the tour turn right along the A487, back towards Caenarfon. About a mile to the north, between Penygroes and Llanwnda is the **Inigo Jones Slateworks** (summer, daily 9am–4.30pm; October to Easter Monday to Friday 9am–4.30pm, Saturday 9am–noon). Here vistors can go on self-guided tours of the workshops and browse in the showroom for a variety of slate souvenirs.

Crafts at Inigo Jones Slateworks

Route 5

Mist at Porth Dinllaen

The Lleyn Peninsula

Criccieth – Pwllheli – Abersoch – Aberdaron – Porth Dinllaen – Llanaelhaearn – Criccieth (75 miles/121km)
See map on pages 30–1

It is hard to look at a map of the Lleyn Peninsula and not to be reminded of Cornwall. The western Lleyn has even been dubbed the 'Land's End of North Wales'. But over the centuries it has suffered none of Cornwall's intensive exploitation for mineral ores and china-clay. Neither has it sustained so many pressures in more recent times from the holiday industry. A scattering of modest resorts Lleyn may have – Criccieth, Pwllheli, Abersoch, Nefyn – but elsewhere the landscape is obstructively hilly and agricultural. One senses in the walled pastures and isolated farmsteads a foreign-ness reminiscent of Brittany, perhaps, or southwest Ireland.

Lleyn's roads were not built for motor traffic. Narrow and twisting, they meander between high banks and tall hedges with occasional sudden views of a shapely hillside or the glint of sunshine on waves.

The remote coastline is a mostly unspoilt Area of Outstanding Natural Beauty, alternating between savage cliffs and golden sands whose inaccessibility guarantees seclusion. From a distance, the Lleyn Peninsula appears disproportionately mountainous. In fact, its hills are not lofty by Snowdonia standards (the highest being around 1,800ft/ 560m) but their presence is accentuated by proximity to the sea. Several hilltops reveal signs of occupation in Celtic times. And at the western tip, across 2 miles (3km) of turbulent tidal race, sits Ynys Enlli ('Isle of Tides') or Bardsey Island – an ancient place of pilgrimage.

Sun at Abersoch

Bardsey Island

Criccieth's central green imparts an intimate village flavour to this essentially family resort. Almost dividing the town into two halves, ★★ **Criccieth Castle** (Easter to end-September, daily 10am–6pm; October to Easter 9.30am–4pm) perches on a grassy headland between a pebble strand backed by hotel terraces on Marine Drive and, to the east, a great arc of safe bathing beach and promenade. Visit the castle ruin if you can, both for its chequered history and for the magnificent views. Built by the Welsh in the 13th century, contemporary with Llywelyn the Great, it was taken by Edward I and incorporated into his 'Iron Ring' of coastal fortifications in 1283. Owain Glyndwr's Welsh uprising besieged and sacked the castle 140 years later, leaving it much as we find it today.

Take the A497 coast road past Llanystumdwy with its

Lloyd George Museum:
an era recreated

★★ **Lloyd George Museum** (daily Easter to October 10am– 5pm), entirely devoted to the life and times of this great Liberal politician. He came to the village after his father died when he was a small child, and lived with his mother in Highgate Cottage opposite the Feathers Inn until 1880. His uncle's shoemaking workshop next door has been imaginatively recreated. Winston Churchill said of Lloyd George: 'He was the greatest Welshman which that unconquerable race has produced since the age of the Tudors.'

Between here and Pwllheli lies **Butlins Starcoast World** holiday complex (daily April to October and March weekends 10am–10pm), open to casual visitors in addition to the resident 'campers'. Beyond, road and railway skirt Morfa Abererch to arrive at **Pwllheli**, largest of the Lleyn's settlements and a market town since 1355. Its inner harbour, once busy with trading vessels, is now silted up, replaced by pleasure craft in the outer harbour area (boat trips). **Glan-y-don beach**, stretching for over 3 miles (5km) from east of the harbour to Pen-ychain, offers the best bathing here on the Lleyn's south coast. Pwllheli is the northern terminus of the scenic ★ **Cambrian Coast Railway** which extends down to Aberystwyth.

Sands run south to ★ **Abersoch**, set in a bay called St Tudwal's Road. This and the two uninhabited offshore islands take their name from a 6th-century Brittany saint who fled from religious persecution in the Dark Ages and founded a monastic cell on St Tudwal's Island East. Ruins of an 800-year-old chapel there can be seen from boat trips around the islands (weather permitting). In Abersoch itself will be found the Lleyn Peninsula's only dyed-in-the-wool holiday resort. A lively harbour, fine beach, narrow shop-lined streets, restaurants, pubs and hotels, as well as extensive complexes of caravans and chalets, all betray a wide appeal.

Head southwest on the unclassified road over to the southern end of **Porth Neigwl** ('Hell's Mouth') above which stands the little village of **Llanengan**. The unrestored, twin-naved ★ **Parish Church** dates from the 15th century, with roots almost a thousand years earlier. Its bells and sacred vessels were brought over from St Mary's Abbey on Bardsey Island whose pilgrims would have called at Llanengan on their journey west.

Taking the northbound by-road across the Afon Soch leads to pretty **Llangian** hamlet. The churchyard contains a 5th- or 6th-century Roman stone bearing an inscription in Latin which declares that the remains of 'Melius the Doctor, son of Martinus, lie here'. In the whole of Britain there is no other record of an early Christian burial mentioning the deceased's profession.

Bear left and left again to the northern end of Hell's Mouth, its anglicised name testimony to the threat this vast crescent bay once posed to sailing ships which risked being driven ashore in southwesterly gales. Ahead there is a steep climb to **Rhiw**, highest village on the Lleyn, where stands a delightful 17th-century Welsh manor house surrounded by its own grounds and ornamental garden. ★ **Plas yn Rhiw** is owned by the National Trust (Easter to May daily 12–5pm except Tuesdays and Wednesdays; May to September closed Tuesdays).

Plas yn Rhiw gardens

39

Three miles (5km) farther west the attractive little fishing village of ★ **Aberdaron** nestles in a fold at the back of its cliff-girt bay, sheltered from all winds but the south. In good weather there are boat trips to view Bardsey Island. The final resting place for 14th-century pilgrims en route for Bardsey was Aberdaron's **Y-Gegin-Fawr** ('The Big Kitchen') near the old hump-backed bridge; it is now a café-cum-gift shop. Recently constructed sea defences paint a vivid picture of Aberdaron's vulnerability to marine erosion. Note how the Norman doorway of **St Hywyn's Church** has been weathered by centuries of storms. When built some 500 years ago it was set back at a safe distance from the shore but now its cemetery rises incongruously from the beach and the building only survives thanks to the provision of its own sea wall.

Y-Gegin-Fawr in Aberdaron

Tentacle-like, single track lanes reach out towards 'land's end'. For a path to the shore go via **Uwchmynydd** to the end of the public road beneath the rocky fist of Mynydd Mawr. Alternatively drive on up the concrete track to old coastguard buildings on the 524-ft (160-m) summit. All around the tip of the Lleyn are uninterrupted views to **Bardsey Island**. Founded in the 6th century, the Abbey of St Mair (St Mary) was a place of pilgrimage for hundreds of years. Many holy men stayed on and were buried there, giving rise to the title 'Island of 20,000

Weatherboarding by the coast

Tre'r Ceiri: summit and sheep

Saints'. During the early 1900s Bardsey was still inhabited by a fishing and farming community but today it is largely a seabird sanctuary, visited by occasional boatloads of ornithologists bound for the observatory. The abbey ruins lie beneath 548-ft (167-m) Mynydd Enlli, roughly in line with the lighthouse. Also in view from high ground are Cardigan Bay down to St David's Head, the Snowdonia peaks and even, appropriately for their shared Celtic heritage, the Wicklow Mountains of Ireland.

Return to Aberdaron and follow the B4413 northeast to **Pen-y-groeslon**. Here turn left on the B4417 to **Tudweilog**. Continue along the B4417 to Morfa Nefyn and walk the mile or so of track to ★ **Porth Dinllaen**, one of the National Trust's most recent acquisitions. The picturesque sandy cove backed by neat cottages and a waterfront pub had once been earmarked as the packet port for Ireland. In 1806 William Madocks, Member of Parliament for Boston, Lincolnshire, formed a company to build a harbour at Porth Dinllaen, but two years later when the necessary Parliamentary bill was introduced it failed to gain support and Holyhead was selected instead. Madocks's ambition resurfaced in 1844 when Porth Dinllaen established its own railway company. However, the Chester and Holyhead line, already built, proved the decisive factor in the final abandonment of Madocks's scheme and Porth Dinllaen sank into quiet obscurity. How different things might have been! Only Madocks's straight road to Pwllheli, designed for speeding transit of the Irish mail, and his development of Porthmadog and Tremadog as staging posts on the route to London (*see Route 3*) remain.

Continue on the B4417 through Nefyn to Llithfaen. A mile (1.6km) to the north at **Nant Gwrtheryn**, Wales' National Language Centre is housed in a once-derelict quarry village, even today a wild and remote spot. **Llanaelhaearn** is a small village at the foot of Lleyn's three most distinctive peaks known as ★ **Yr Eifl** ('The Forks'), or by their English name **The Rivals**. The highest, central top reaches 1,850ft (564m), the lowest, to seaward, 1,457ft (444m). But it is the eastern peak that holds the greatest interest for its summit is crowned by the remains of ★ **Tre'r Ceiri** ('Town of the Giants'). This ancient fortified settlement, probably of Bronze Age origin and containing well-preserved hut circles, can be reached by a footpath off the B4417 less than a mile southwest of Llanaelhaearn.

Take the southbound A499 and in almost 4 miles (6km) turn left onto the B4354 through **Chwilog**, part of Madocks' proposed London to Porth Dinllaen turnpike which he claimed would have been 30 miles (48km) shorter than the route to Holyhead.

Route 6

Ardudwy: Tremadog Bay to the Mawddach Estuary

Porthmadog – Portmeirion – Harlech – Barmouth – Llanelltyd – Trawsfynydd – Porthmadog (53 miles/85km) *See map on pages 30–31*

Ardudwy, the high and ancient upland region between the Vale of Ffestiniog and the Mawddach estuary, guards its secrets well. Many of the *Mabinogion's* heroic sagas are based here and there is a sense of Ireland too, just across the glittering sea, in the primeval stones named *cyttiau wyddelod* – 'Irishman's huts'. Old drovers' roads with their robust drystone walls climbing the glaciated humps and hollows were in use until the railways took over livestock transportation in the late 19th century. Modern roads only tickle the foothills. It is rough country to walk in, perhaps the roughest in all Snowdonia. In his book *On Foot in North Wales*, published in 1933, Patrick Monkhouse writes about an ascent of Rhinog Fawr: 'it exacts more perspiration to the yard than any other mile in Wales…' Fortunately the coastline is a softer place by far, with dunes and sandy beaches extending all the way down to Barmouth, and Harlech Castle jutting defiantly skyward in distant views.

Cwm Bychan in the Rhinogs

Shortly after crossing ★ **The Cob** (small toll) from **Porthmadog** (*see Route 3, page 27*) take the driveway on the right to ★★★ **Portmeirion** (daily 9.30am–5.30pm), a folly *par excellence* which draws in visitors from across the globe. Following a tour of Italy when he became captivated by the fishing village of Portofino, the architect Clough Williams-Ellis searched for a suitable site on which

The Rhinogs from Portmeirion

Portmeirion detail

The toll bridge

View from Llandecwyn Church

to create an Italianate fantasy of his own. In 1925, quite by chance, he was offered the present land, then derelict, beside the Dwyryd estuary not far from his ancestral home. His declared mission was to 'show that one could develop even a very beautiful place without defiling it and, given sufficient care, you could even enhance what was given as a backdrop'. Williams-Ellis always intended Portmeirion to awaken visitors' interest in architecture, decor and landscaping. In amongst the extravaganza of small-scale, pastel-coloured Mediterranean buildings, including shops and a restaurant, appear architectural oddments from all over Britain, some rescued from demolition sites by Williams-Ellis himself.

The 19th-century house standing on the original site became the Portmeirion Hotel which hosted many celebrities during the 1930s. Bernard Shaw and John Steinbeck stayed there, as did the playwright Noel Coward to write *Blithe Spirit*. Portmeirion was the main location for *The Prisoner* TV series. There are walks above the sandy shoreline backed by subtropical gardens as well as through woodland to little bays on the peninsula's south side. (NB: Strong tidal currents make bathing dangerous.)

Return to the A497 and fork right opposite Penrhyndeudraeth's church to pass the railway station on the scenic ★ **Cambrian Coast Line** between Pwllheli and Aberystwyth. In fact, the road curves across the Afon Dwyryd beside the railway line on a **toll bridge** to Llandecwyn station before heading for the lake-dotted foothills north of the main Rhinog range, encountered more closely later. Rather than following the A496 south, stay on this by-road via **Bryn Bwbach**. Up to the left, halfway between the two Tecwyn lakes, stands the isolated little ★ **Llandecwyn Church**, also a magnificent viewpoint. Resuming south-

erly progress, fork right after a couple of miles at **Eisin-grug** to reach the B4573. Alternatively, for superb panoramas over Tremadog Bay, stay on the narrow mountain road climbing the shoulder of **Moel Goedog**, 1,211ft (369m), an area rich in prehistoric remains. Either way, the next port of call will be Harlech.

★★★ **Harlech Castle** (Easter to late October daily 9.30am–6.30pm; November to Easter 9.30am–4pm and 11am–4pm Sunday) entirely dominates the little hillside town. Its square-cut profile atop a 200-ft (60-m) high crag is visible from many miles distant. James of St George, Edward I's Master of Works during the construction of North Wales's mighty coastal fortresses, became Constable of Harlech in 1290. Under his direction, Harlech Castle was given four massive towers, anchoring the great curtain walls. A huge gatehouse, rather than the more usual central keep, formed the building's strongest section. The Castle's position directly above a tidal creek (the sea has since receded about ½ mile/800m) permitted victualling from the sea, and supplies from

Aspects of Harlech Castle

Ireland were carried up the west side steps which still exist today. Despite its apparent impregnability, the Castle fell to Owain Glyndwr in 1404, though it was recaptured by the English within five years and went on to feature in the Wars of the Roses when the siege (and subsequent surrender) of the Lancastrian garrison inspired the now famous marching song *Men of Harlech*.

Harlech overlooks 5 miles (8km) of dune-backed sandy beach and a vast expanse of reclaimed land – **Morfa Harlech** – part of which is a nature reserve. Nearer the town will be found car parking, campsites and other holiday development.

In complete contrast, a narrow mountain road to the east snakes uphill into ★ **Cwm Bychan** where, from the road-end car park, an ascent may be made to the so-called **Roman Steps**. (Research suggests the paved way is more likely to have been a medieval packhorse route.) Rhinog terrain – rocks and boulders concealed beneath deep heather – is notoriously rugged. Any attempt to scale **Rhinog Fawr**, 2,362ft (720m), should only be made by experienced and well-equipped hillwalkers. These are, however, splendidly wild hills, a landscape of boggy hollows, bare cliffs, knobbly ridge crests and high, lonely lakes. Only two ways cross the range – Bwlch Tyddiad with its Roman steps and Bwlch Drws Ardudwy to the south. The Reverend W. Bingley, writing in the late 18th century, found the latter pass: 'a place well calculated to inspire a timid mind with terror' – and certainly in poor weather it can be an intimidating place.

South of Harlech, a right turn off the A496 at Llanfair leads to the 4th-century ★ **Llandanwg Church**. Long

Shell seekers

since unused and invaded by drifting dunes, this is one of the very earliest places of worship in Wales. From Llanbedr a tidal causeway leads out to ★ **Shell Island (Mochras)**, an exposed, low-lying peninsula with a camp-site, marina and over 200 varieties of shell deposited by unusual offshore currents. Inland, again, another narrow mountain road with picnic spots approaches the Rhinogs via **Cwm Nantcol**.

Never far from the railway line, the A496 proceeds south past Dyffryn Ardudwy and Tal-y-bont, nudged ever nearer the sandy shore by high ground until from **Llan-aber** everything crowds cheek-by-jowl into the only us-able corridor of land.

Barmouth harbour

Barmouth's Welsh name, Abermaw, a contraction of Aber-mawddach ('Estuary of the Mawddach'), dates back to its humble origins as a fishing port and boatyard. When the railway came in the mid-19th century, the village's ex-tensive sandy beach and its incomparable views over the estuary to Cadair Idris quickly earned it a reputation as a holiday resort.

Four and a half acres (1.8 hectares) of cliffland above the town – **Dinas Oleu ('Fortress of Light')** – repre-sents the National Trust's very first acquisition; it was pre-sented by Mrs F. Talbot in 1895, the year of the Trust's foundation, and a further 12 acres (4.8 hectares) were added to it in 1980. It is well signposted and a little fur-ther east will be found the waymarked ★★ **Panorama Walk** providing views not only of Cadair Idris and the coast but inland over the estuary's head to the distant Aran mountains. It is also possible to cross the railway line's timber viaduct spanning the Mawddach (always a vul-nerable section of the Cambrian Coast Line and expensive to maintain) using the ★ **pedestrian walkway**. Additional-ly a seasonal ferry runs across to the narrow-gauge Fair-bourne Railway on the far shore (*see Route 9, page 56*).

In this region of mid-Wales the happy juxtaposition of railway stations and superb walking country opens up numerous possibilities for returning to the start of rambles by train.

Just in from Barmouth Harbour (boat trips) stands **Ty Crwn**, a circular 'lock-up' built in the early 1800s to ac-commodate, among other offenders, drunken goldmin-ers from the Bontddu area just upstream.

The Ty Crwn lock-up

In June of each year Barmouth sees the start of the Three Peaks International Yacht Race during which competitors sail to Fort William, climbing en route to the summits of Snowdon, Scafell Pike and Ben Nevis. And if the resort's present-day ambience is of 'sandcastles, donkey rides and candy floss', at least there is ample car parking and plenty of space for everyone.

The A496 now traces the tree-clad northern shore of the **Afon Mawddach** and into former gold territory. The Welsh Gold Rush began around 1850 with the discovery of the precious yellow metal at Clogau on the western edge of the so-called Dolgellau Gold Belt which stretched in a wide arc from Bala in the east to **Bontddu** on the Mawddach estuary. After a highly profitable period during 1904–6, production steadily declined and Clogau closed in 1911. The fenced-off entrance to the Clogau St David's gold mine can still be seen today, to the west of a lane running up from Bontddu beside the Hirgwm stream. The wedding rings of the Queen Mother (1923), the Queen (1947), Princess Margaret (1960), Princess Anne (1973) and Diana, Princess of Wales (1981) were all crafted from the same nugget of Welsh gold found there.

Near Llanelltyd the **New Precipice Walk** skirts the slopes of Foel Ispri 1,000ft (300m) above the Afon Mawddach. The better known **Precipice Walk** begins further east from car parking near Llyn Cynwch (*see Route 8, page 53*). See also the modest but evocative remains nearby of **Cymmer Abbey** (open daily; tickets at adjacent farmhouse), founded in 1199 and one of the major Cistercian foundations supported by the Princes of Gwynedd. The ruins are mainly those of the uncompleted 13th-century abbey church.

Mountain rescue above Bontddu

Cymmer Abbey

Across the river to the right stands Dolgellau, but the A470 forks left at Llanelltyd and climbs back to the north and towards the starting point of the route through the **Coed-y-Brenin**. More details on this magnificent forest are given in Route 8 (*see pages 53–4*), but even if you're only passing it's still well worth calling in at the **Maesgwm Visitor Centre** to the left of the main road.

The road strikes due north to by-pass **Trawsfynydd** village, with the Rhinog mountains – the heights of Ardudwy – ranged along the western skyline. Bwlch Drws Ardudwy forms a conspicuous notch, while the highest top, Y Llethr (1,875ft/756m) lies at the southern end of the massif. At Llyn Trawsfynydd, the **Magnox Nuclear Power Station** (daily 9.30am–4.30pm; hourly guided tours; free admission but book in advance during the high season), its waters once warmed by the reactors, is undergoing decommissioning. Several nature trails have been established around the complex.

Ignore the A470's right turn to Ffestiniog and branch left at **Gellilydan** on a by-road over to **Maentwrog** in the beautiful Vale of Ffestiniog (*see Route 3, page 28*). Parallel to the Ffestiniog Railway which threads unseen but often heard through the forest above, the A487 heads towards Porthmadog via **Penrhyndeudraeth**, headquarters of the Snowdonia National Park.

The road across the Migneint

Route 7

Bala and Environs

Bala – (Llanuwchllyn – Dolhendre – Trawsfynydd) – Llyn Celyn – Ffestiniog – The Migneint – Bala *See map on pages 30–31*

Away from centres of population, tourist attractions and Snowdonia's most popularised mountains, there is an unexpected wildness reminiscent of the northern Pennines. Villages and farmsteads cling to the edges of this 'empty quarter'. Mist often clings to its high ground, adding moisture to an already wet landscape of bog and lakes, of tumbling streams and waterfalls. Exploration on foot is not easy but a few mountain roads do transect the area, providing an opportunity to experience the roof of Snowdonia from the security of a vehicle.

Bala Lake

Bala Lake (Llyn Tegid) constitutes the largest natural area of water in Wales, being about 4½ miles (7km) long by ⅔ mile (1km) wide and with a maximum depth of 136ft (48m). Because of its situation in the great rift valley extending southwest to Tal-y-Llyn and the sea at Tywyn – a natural through-route from the Vale of Chester – many travellers have written of the lake, its susceptibility to flooding in southwesterly gales, its prodigious fish population (including the unique alpine gwyniad) and the fine sailing to be had upon its waters. **Bala** town, prior to the Industrial Revolution, became a prosperous centre of the woollen industry. Thomas Pennant wrote of women and children 'in full employ, knitting along the roads'. However, Bala's reputation as a religious centre proved more enduring. There is a town-centre **statue to Thomas**

Statue of Thomas Charles, Bala

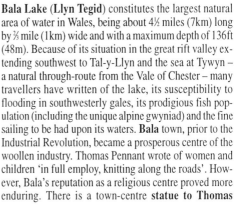

Charles, pioneer of Welsh Calvinistic Methodism and a leader of the Sunday School movement.

Hauled by narrow-gauge steam and diesel engines, the **Bala Lake Railway** (Easter to end-September, daily 10am–5pm), carries visitors along the scenic eastern shore of the lake to and from **Llanuwchllyn**, closely accompanied by the B4403. The village was the birthplace of Michael Jones, a prominent Welsh Nationalist who initiated Welsh settlement in Patagonia.

To the southeast of Llanuwchllyn, an impressive mountain road climbs to Bwlch y Groes, Wales's highest road pass at 1,790ft (546m), giving access to the mighty Aran Mountains before dropping to Dinas Mawddwy *(see Route 8, page 52)*. A similarly high-level road heads east from Llanuwchllyn. At **Pen-y-bont**, 300m after joining the northbound A494, turn left beside the Afon Lliw. In about 1½ miles (2.5km) the road crosses the river at **Dolhendre** and begins a long ascent into wild open country before re-crossing the Afon Lliw to reach its highest point at 1,742ft (531m) above sea level. Travellers should note, however that, while spectacular, the route does involve the opening and closing of numerous gates. Passing through forestry and accompanying the Afon Gain for a mile or so lower down, the route swings northwest to meet the A470 near **Trawsfynydd** *(see Route 6, page 45)*.

A much easier road to the east, also joining the A470 near Trawsfynydd, is the A4212 from Bala, via Llyn Celyn. Just beyond the junction with the B4501 at Fron-goch, to the left of the main road, is the **National White Water Centre**, where, on Saturdays and Sundays, the experts can be seen negotiating the rapids of the Afon Tryweryn. Normally reduced to a mere trickle by the dam of Llyn Celyn above, there is a 'release' of water every weekend. Competitions are held about once a month.

Not so many years ago Llyn Celyn itself was just a marshy valley containing the long established community of Capel Celyn and the old railway line from Blaenau Ffestiniog to Bala. During the 1960s – a time of momentous environmental decisions, not least the building of Trawsfynydd nuclear power station – the Afon Tryweryn was dammed to form Llyn Celyn as a holding reservoir for Liverpool Corporation. The drowned village with its complement of Quakers, many of whom subsequently emigrated to Pennsylvania, is remembered by a bronze plaque set on a boulder just beyond the grass-covered dam and in a newly restored **chapel** at the lake's northwestern end. There is fishing in the lake and a number of parking laybys off the A4212.

A mile beyond the decommissioned nuclear power station on the shore of Llyn Trawsfynydd, turn right with the A470

Waterfall en route from Dolhendre

47

Expert manoeuvres at the National White Water Centre

The 'Swampy Place'

Ysbyty Ifan

Snowdonia from the B5421

towards **Ffestiniog**, a large village of terraced stone houses situated some way south of the main slate quarries which take its name. Blaenau Ffestiniog lies 3 miles (5km) to the north *(see Route 3, page 28)*. From near the old railway station a footpath leads to the delightful ★ **Rhaeadr Cynfal**, or the **Cynfal Falls**. Another fine waterfall on the Afon Cynfal – **Rhaeadr y Cwm** – can be reached on foot 1½ miles (2.5km) upstream from Bont Newydd where the A470 bends sharply left to cross the river.

At Ffestiniog turn right onto the B4391, the old, pre-power station road from Porthmadog to Bala. Soon after passing a superb viewpoint into the Cynfal ravine, take a left turn onto the B4407. In every direction the land rolls out into bog and heather moorland. This is the **Migneint** ('Swampy Place'). The often saturated hillsides of reeds and peat hags, where acid ground has encouraged the growth of mat-grass, cotton-grass and deer's hair-sedge, represent the most significant area of such terrain in Wales. Walkers venturing forth have to contend with pools of black water, very soggy going and in all likelihood the need to navigate by compass in the frequent mists. Little wonder it is so little visited. Nevertheless the Migneint is extremely important ecologically. Large tracts have been acquired by the National Trust and designated a Grade 1 Site of Special Scientific Interest.

The ribbon of tarmac winds over this desolate, lake-dotted wilderness, home to snipe, grouse and curlew, and in about 3 miles (5km), at **Pont ar Conwy**, crosses the infant River Conwy not far from its source in Llyn Conwy. To the southeast rises the peak of Arenig Fach (2,261ft/ 689m) while downstream is encountered the sleepy village of **Ysbyty Ifan**, centre of the National Trust's large Penrhyn Estate.

Fork right on an unclassified road over the River Conwy, continuing to **Pentrefoelas** on the A5. From here, on a clear day, visitors are strongly recommended to take a short detour to the north along the B5113. After the village of **Nebo**, the B5421 branches off to Llanrwst *(see Route 1, page 17)*, but just beyond this fork in the road is a lay-by offering stunning ★★ **views** down into the Conwy Valley and up to the distant summits of Snowdonia, the outlines of the mountains and their deep U-shaped valleys clearly etched against the western skies.

Back on the A5, by-pass **Rhydlydan** and, temporarily leaving the National Park, continue to **Cerrigydrudion**. One mile (1.6km) south of the village turn right onto the B4501 Bala road. Once across the Afon Ceirw it climbs over to the Afon Medrad valley before swinging west and south to Fron-goch and Bala.

Route 8

The Aran Mountains from Bwlch y Groes

Dolgellau to Cadair Idris and the Aran Mountains

Dolgellau – Minffordd – Corris – Dyfi Valley – Dinas Mawddwy – Bwlch y Groes – Llanfachreth – Coed-y-Brenin *See map on pages 30–31*

Dolgellau, slightly offset from the great Bala–Talyllyn geological fault line, stands near the southern entrance to Snowdonia. Apart from Cadair Idris, Snowdon's equivalent in the popularity stakes, less familiar country stretches southeast to the beautiful valley of the River Dyfi (often anglicised to Dovey). The vast Dyfi Forest, threaded by old slate-mining tracks, spreads its mantle of conifers over a complex, folded landscape. Some of the hilltops sport wind turbines, for this is 'alternative technology' territory. To the east of Dolgellau, the volcanic Aran mountains extend from Dinas Mawddwy to Bala Lake, only failing by a whisker to reach the magic 3,000ft but nevertheless boasting Wales's highest road. To the north lies the Coed-y-Brenin Forest, where larch and Sitka spruce clothe a hilly landscape whose streams all flow into the Mawddach; it is an area of waterfalls, abandoned gold and copper mines and numerous forest trails, ideal for walkers and mountain-bikers.

Alternative technology country

For centuries ★ **Dolgellau** has provided hospitality for travellers and it remains a great favourite with visitors today. In the early 1400s Owain Glyndwr held parliament here but the town's main significance revolved around its great sheep and cattle fairs. Livestock are still brought in for the weekly market and there is a major summer agricultural show. The town's mostly 19th-century Market Square area of pale granite buildings is less both-

Dolgellau

ered by traffic than it once was thanks to the road by-pass, but it is still a busy place. Narrow, irregular streets lined with shops and restaurants invite browsing while to the north, not far from the Parish Church with its medieval tower and excellent Victorian stained glass, a seven-arched bridge (Bont Fawr) spans the Afon Wnion. There is an interesting **Meirioneth Quaker Museum** above the Tourist Information Centre (daily 10am–1pm and 2–6pm; closed winter Tuesdays and Wednesdays).

Follow the A470 east up to **Cross Foxes** and bear right onto the A487. High mountain country lies ahead and from the pass (Bwlch Talyllyn) at 938ft (286m) there are stunning views down the crag-bound upper valley here on the Bala–Talyllyn fault line (the largest land-shift in Wales) running northeast to southwest through southern Snowdonia. **Tal-y-llyn Lake** gleams in the distance while up to the right rear the outlying flanks of ★ **Cadair Idris** ('Chair of Idris'). This volcanic massif, eroded by aeons of glacial action into a peak of savage beauty, is named after Idris, a local hero killed in battle against the Saxons around AD630. Tradition decrees that anyone sleeping overnight in the 'chair' (its precise position is unclear) will wake as either a lunatic or a poet.

Park at **Minffordd** for an ascent from the south via the lovely Llyn Cau to Penygadair, Cadair Idris's highest top at 2,930ft (893m). However, bear in mind that it is a steep and very rough climb, as serious as Snowdon but without trains or a café on top. Interestingly, during the late 19th century one Richard Pugh of Dolgellau did construct a stone hut on the summit in which he provided visitors with 'all convenient refreshments while waiting for the dispersion of the misty clouds in order to enjoy the exquisite prospect…' Pugh's hut remains, now down-

Autumm colours at Minffordd and Llyn Cau on Cadair Idris

graded to a basic shelter but welcome nonetheless. (For Cadair Idris from the north, *see Route 9*).

Less than a mile (1.3km) southwest of Minffordd on the B4405, cradled by sweeping mountainsides, stretch the waters of ★ **Tal-y-llyn Lake** (or, to give it its true Welsh name, Llyn Mwyngil – 'Lake in the Pleasant Retreat'). It is indeed a peaceful lake, shallow but abundant in fish and flora, notably its yellow water-lily. From the handsome Tyn-y-Cornel Hotel, and the adjacent little unspoilt church, a lakeside track along the north shore provides an easy and pleasant walk to Minffordd.

The A487 Machynlleth road continues towards Corris, but most visitors first call at **Corris Craft Centre**, a purpose-built, modernist complex of studios in which craftspeople can be watched making pottery, toys, leatherware, jewellery and candles. There is also a restaurant and ★ **King Arthur's Labyrinth** (April to end-October, daily 10am–5pm). Access is by boat through a magic waterfall in subterranean caverns where some of the Welsh legends pertaining to King Arthur are explored in tableaux with stunning light and sound effects. **Corris** itself, east

Keeping time in Corris

51

off the main road, stands amidst the convoluted, timber-clad hills of ★ **Dyfi Forest**. The village grew up around slate quarrying in the Afon Dulas valley and a narrow-gauge railway was built in 1859 to transport slate down to the main line at Machynlleth. Steam locomotives replaced horses in 1879. For more details of this and the Corris Railway Society's restoration work visit the **Railway Museum** (daily Easter week then Whitsun to end-September, 1–5pm). As well as a Heritage Trail north of the village, there are forest trails suitable for walking and cycling further up the Dulas valley around Aberllefenni.

Signed to the left off a bend in the descending A487 road is one of southern Snowdonia's most compelling visitor attractions. The ★★★ **Centre for Alternative Technology** (daily 10am–6pm or dusk if earlier; Cliff Railway Easter to end-October) was developed from modest beginnings in the early 1970s at a disused slate quarry near the hamlet of Pantperthog. Its ethos is to demonstrate the effectiveness of alternative energy sources, house insulation and organic food production. By examining such technologies as solar, wind and wave power, house building and sustainable soil fertilisation, the centre challenges in a thought-provoking and entertaining way conventional views about how an advanced industrial society should utilise its resources. The CAT provides a great day out for all ages. Entry is by water-powered cliff railway and within the 7 acres (2.8 hectares) will be found hands-on displays, organic gardens, animals and beehives, a vegetarian restaurant, a bookshop and much else.

Experimenting at the CAT

Both the main A487 road and a parallel lane on the east bank of the Afon Dulas descend into the lovely ★ **Dyfi (Dovey) Valley**. Traditionally the frontier between north and south Wales, this is the modern-day meeting place of Gwynedd, Powys and Ceredigion. Across the Afon Dyfi stands Machynlleth, a colourful, bustling market town with many interesting features *(see Route 9, page 59)*.

Turn left on the B4404 past Llanwin and stay on the northwest bank of the Dyfi on an unclassified road all the way to **Aberangell** and **Minllyn**, small villages on the eastern fringe of Dyfi Forest. On the skyline of Mynydd y Cemais to the southeast are ranged wind turbines belonging to the CAT's wind farm. The road closely shadows the dismantled Mawddwy Railway which, in the mid-1800s connected Dinas Mawddwy with the main Cambrian Railway at Cemmaes Road 7 miles (11km) to the south. Passenger services ceased in 1930 but the line was kept open for goods traffic until damage to a bridge over the Dyfi closed it more conclusively in 1951. Ever-industrious, the Victorians had planned to extend the Mawddwy line north to join the Great Western Railway at Llanuwchllyn *(see Route 7, page 47)* by tunnelling beneath the Aran mountains. Unfortunately the project's sponsor, local landowner Sir Edmund Buckley, was declared bankrupt in 1876 before work began. To the left near **Pont Minllyn**, a 17th-century packhorse bridge, stands **Meirion Mill** (March to October, daily 10am–5pm), a woollen shop set in the old Dinas Mawddwy station buildings, but no longer a functioning woollen mill.

Dinas Mawddwy

★ **Dinas Mawddwy** itself was described by George Borrow in *Wild Wales* (published in 1862) as 'little more than a collection of filthy huts… Fierce-looking red-haired banditti of old were staggering about, and sounds of drunken revelry echoed from the huts…' Dinas, however, had once been a much more important place, with over 1,000 inhabitants, shops, inns, several fairs and major cattle sales. Later prosperity came from lead mining and slate quarrying. Today the village, snug in an amphitheatre of wooded and rhododendron-clad hills at the confluence of the Dyfi and Cerist rivers, enjoys a more peaceful existence as a walking centre.

To the north lie the volcanic **Aran Mountains**, which extend to Bala Lake and culminate in **Aran Fawddwy** (2,976ft/907m). To explore the Aran ridge, drive northeast to **Aber-Cywarch** and there turn left to ★ **Cwm Cywarch**. Following access problems in the 1980s, the Arans are regaining their popularity, but keep to the concessionary paths and heed the 'No Dogs' signs. Being properly equipped and choosing favourable weather become even more vital in remote hills such as these. As a further detour to the route, the unclassified mountain road continues beside the Afon Dyfi to **Llanymawd-dwy**, shortly beyond which the river is crossed and the scenery grows appreciably wilder by the minute. Precipitous slopes up to 1,000ft (300m) high, deeply scarred by stream beds, crowd in ahead. The road is correspondingly steep as it climbs the tributary valley of the Afon Rhiwlech, passes a right fork to Lake Vyrnwy and reaches ★★ **Bwlch y Groes**, 1,791ft (485m) above sea level. There is car parking here at Wales's highest road pass and views extend north towards the Arenig mountains and west to the Arans – a truly spectacular spot to be attained by vehicle. The road descends to **Llanuwch-llyn**, not far from the southern end of Bala Lake (*see Route 7, page 47*), from where you can join the A494 back to Dolgellau.

Bwlch y Groes

A direct return to Dolgellau from Dinas Mawddwy can be made on the A470. Ascending the Cerist valley to **Bwlch Oerddrws** ('Cold Door Pass') at 1,178ft (359m), it skirts scenic cwms and waterfalls. Beyond the pass there are magnificent views of Cadair Idris.

After passing Cross Foxes once again, about 2½ miles (4km) before reaching Dolgellau, turn sharp right onto the B4416 to **Brithdir**. A mile before the village, car parking on the left marks the start of the popular ★ **Torrent Walk**. Under a mile (1km) in length, the path's best stretch drops through beautiful deciduous woodland beside a series of waterfalls in the fast-flowing Afon Clywedog.

Continue on the B4416 to **Bont Newydd**, and almost opposite the junction with the A494, follow the narrow, twisting lane to the tiny settlement of **Llanfachreth**. (A wider unclassified road reaches here from Dolgellau via the slopes of Foel Offrwm.)

The best known ★★ **Precipice Walk**, and the first to be established in the Snowdonia region, begins a mile (1.6km) southwest of Llanfachreth from roadside car parking. Much of the 3½-mile (5.5-km) circular walk, which takes in lovely **Llyn Cynwch** and stunning views over the Mawddach estuary, is easy and intrinsically safe. In places, however, it does traverse very steep hillside. The path is not a public right-of-way, instead enjoying concessionary status since 1890, courtesy of the Nannau Estate.

Llanfachreth nestles at the southern edge of the magnificent ★ **Coed-y-Brenin** ('The King's Forest'), so named after George V's Silver Jubilee in 1935. Despite impressive commercial statistics (nearly 22,000 acres – 8,900 hectares – yielding around 40,000 tonnes of timber annually), Coed-y-Brenin remains one of the most varied and lovely forests in Wales. Situated in what used to be Meirioneth, it straddles the rivers Gamlan, Eden, Gain and Wen, along with the Mawddach into which all the oth-

53

Encounters on the Precipice Walk

Mountain bikers at Maesgwm

Glasdir Arboretum

Rhaeadr Du falls

ers flow. Within the forest can be found wooded gorges, crags, waterfalls and boulder-strewn rivers, secluded upland pastures and a scattering of farmsteads. Comprehensive audio-visual displays about the forest's topography, wildlife and management can be enjoyed at ★ **Maesgwm Visitor Centre** (Easter to end-September daily and winter weekends, 10am–5pm), situated to the west of the A470, 8 miles (13km) north of Dolgellau. Pick up details of the many waymarked forest trails; it is possible to plan delightful rambles or mountain bike tours from any of the numerous car parks and picnic areas.

At **Glasdir**, less than a mile west of Llanfachreth on the banks of the tumbling Afon Las, an **Arboretum** of mountain tree species has been established. Further down still are the ruins of **Glasdir Copper Mine** on a trail exploring the remains of 19th-century copper mining in the area. The mineral, present in the rocks and impregnated peat of the Mawddach valley, had probably been extracted since prehistoric times. At the height of its activity, Glasdir Mine, worked by some 160 employees, produced 50 tons of ore per day. The mine finally closed in 1914.

From Glasdir take the left-hand of two parallel lanes dropping to the Afon Wen and cross the river near its confluence with the Afon Eden. In under a mile this forestry by-road crosses the Afon Eden and joins the A470. Ahead at Ganllwyd there is car parking for a short walk west up to ★ **Rhaeadr Du** and a sequence of beautiful waterfalls in the Afon Gamlan.

At the end of the adopted road beside the infant Afon Mawddach river northeast from Ganllwyd (to the east of the A470), a rough track (no vehicles) continues to Bont Gwynfynydd. Here the rivers Mawddach and Gain each roar over their own spectacular waterfalls – ★ **Rhaeadr Mawddach** and ★ **Pistyll Gain** respectively – before joining forces near the site of the old Gwynfynydd Gold Mine. The now derelict mine, which had closed in 1939, was temporarily resurrected in 1985 by a group of three men who managed limited production for four years. However, the fortunes of such small-scale enterprises depend on Welsh gold, distinguished by the 'Welsh Maiden' mark, being in demand for exclusive jewellery.

Parallel to the A470 for some distance to the east lies the course of Sarn Helen, an ancient north to south drove road (though most went east towards Offa's Dyke). It was adapted by the Romans for their own use to link Caerhun, near Conwy (*see Route 1*) with Maridunum (Carmarthen) and can still be traced, intermittently, throughout the entire length of Wales. According to the *Mabinogion* the road was laid in the 4th century AD by Helen, noble bride of the self-styled Emperor Magnus Maximus who was dream-led to Wales by his vision of her.

Route 9

Trippers in Tywyn

Cadair Idris and around the coast to Machynlleth

Dolgellau – Cregennen Lakes – Arthog – Castell y Bere
– Abergynolwyn – Tywyn – Aberdyfi – Machynlleth
(48 miles/78km) *See map on pages 30–31*

55

Between the Mawddach and the Dyfi (Dovey) estuaries
lies a bulge of high land rising to Cadair Idris and split
through the middle by the Bala–Talyllyn geological fault.
Mountain roads probe the heart of this, Snowdonia's most
southerly outpost with its ancient churches, castle ruins,
'Great Little Trains' and links with the legend of King
Arthur. At Fairbourne, Tywyn and Aberdyfi, long sandy
beaches provide the setting for holiday activities without the razzmatazz of more commercially developed resorts. With the southern flanks of Cadair Idris examined
in Route 8, this route sees what the great mountain has
to offer from the north and east, alternating between coast
and foothills to arrive, ultimately, at Machynlleth, the
southernmost gateway to Snowdonia.

*Ancient churches and
Great Little Trains*

Many come to Dolgellau *(see Route 8, page 49)* to explore
around ★ **Cadair Idris** whose craggy northern escarpment
dominates the horizon. Some come to climb it. Already
by the mid-18th century guides were leading visitors to
the 2,930ft (833m) summit of Penygadair. Nowadays so
many tramp up the mountain that footpath erosion is caus-
ing serious problems.

Fork left up the old coaching road, a narrow lane, which
leaves Dolgellau from the west end of Fford Cader Idris
(Cadair Idris Street) and in 1 mile (1.6km) turn right to
pass roadside **Llyn Gwernan**. The well known **Fox's Path**
up Cadair Idris starts here, although its upper reaches be-

yond Llyn y Gadair are so badly eroded as to be quite dangerous. A little further on at the **Ty-Nant** car park begins the **Pony Path** over to Cwm Pennant; from the saddle at its highest point (Rhiw Gwredydd), Cadair Idris's summit, Penygadair, is easily reached.

The road meanders along beneath frowning cliffs rising almost 1,500ft (450m) to Craig-las. About 300m after crossing a cattle grid, turn off right to enjoy the two idyllically situated ★★ **Cregennen lakes** (car parking). They occupy part of a 705-acre (285-hectare) National Trust property donated in 1959 by Major C.L.Wynne-Jones in memory of his two sons killed in World War II. Standing stones marked on the map date from around 1800BC; as with numerous others in Snowdonia their exact purpose is unknown, but they might have been deity symbols, or boundary or route markers. The heights of Cadair Idris loom to the east, with the Mawddach estuary stretching below to the west: glorious views of both can be had from the summit of the easily climbed hill immediately to the north of the lakes.

The Cregennen Lakes

A tortuous descent ensues to reach **Arthog**. Waterfalls punctuate the stream flowing down through the village: few would guess that it rises in the tiniest of glacial corrie lakes – Llyn Cyri – high under Cadair Idris's outlying crags. Passing near Arthog, a 6-mile (9.5-km) long nature trail, established by the RSPB and the North Wales Naturalists' Trust, utilises the trackbed of the old Aberystwyth and Welsh Coast Railway (1865–1965). Called the ★ **Penmaenpool to Morfa Mawddach Walk**, it skirts the estuary's very shoreline and is suitable for walking or cycling.

From **Fairbourne** – mostly modern bungalows – a fascinating 15in (38cm) gauge ★ **Miniature Railway**, horse-drawn until 1916, originally for the conveyance of building materials, runs over a mile (2.2km) out along a duney sandspit to Penrhyn Point. From there, glorious river and mountain views are obtained and there is a seasonal **foot passenger ferry** across to Barmouth *(see Route 6, page 44)*. An alternative crossing of the estuary can be made on the Cambrian Coast railway viaduct which has a ★ **pedestrian walkway** *(see also Route 6, page 44)*.

Llangelynnin Church

One and three-quarter miles (2km) beyond Llwyngwril on the A493 coast road, adjacent to a railway halt, stands ★ **Llangelynnin Church**. Set just above the shingle beach, this primitive, mainly 12th-century building is dedicated to a local 7th-century saint, Celynnin.

Heading south, high coastal hills force the A493 inland although the railway manages to squeeze past. In less than 2 miles (3km) bear left to **Llanegryn**, notable for another extraordinary little ★ **church**. This one sits on hillside half a mile (800m) northwest of the village and reveals a remarkably beautiful Rood-screen and loft, probably carved by local craftsmen in the 15th or early 16th century, or, as tradition has it, brought there from Cymmer Abbey near Dolgellau *(see Route 6, page 45)* at the Reformation.

The Afon Dysynni is crossed opposite the dramatic, soaring buttress of **Craig yr Aderyn** (Birds' Rock), the only inland cormorant nesting site in Britain. Straight over the crossroads, in a wild and romantic setting at the heart of mountainous country and with fabulous views of the western flanks of Cadair Idris, stand the extensive but fragmentary ruins of ★★ **Castell y Bere** (open at all times). Started by Llywelyn the Great around 1221, the fortress guarded southern Meirionydd and the mountain route to Dolgellau. During the early part of 1283 Castell y Bere became one of Prince Dafydd ap Gruffydd's final refuges but was eventually surrendered later that same year to Edward I's 3,000-strong invading army.

Castel y Bere

It was the last Welsh castle to fall. Less than two years later it was re-taken by the Welsh, who destroyed what they could and abandoned the rest to the elements.

57

At the road's end beyond **Llanfihangel-y-pennant**, a monument to Mary Jones has been installed in the ruin of her cottage, **Tyn-y-ddod**. In 1800, aged only 16, she walked barefoot over to Bala (about 26 miles/42km) to buy a Welsh bible from the Methodist minister there, Thomas Charles *(see Route 7, page 46)*. He had none to sell but gave her his own. Mary's zeal for the scriptures so impressed him that he began a campaign from which grew the British and Foreign Bible Society. From the adjacent road-end begins the **Pony Path** over the shoulder of Cadair Idris to Dolgellau, a more gentle though longer approach to the mountain than other paths.

Return to the crossroads and bear left to **Abergynolwyn**. Once an important slate quarrying centre, the village nestles in the Dysynni valley surrounded by forestry. Here, short of Tal-y-llyn lake itself *(see Route 8, page 51)*, stands Nant Gwernol Station (forest walks but no road access), northern terminus of the famous 2ft 3in (68cm) gauge ★★★ **Talyllyn Railway** (daily February to October but consult timetable). The line is the oldest of its kind in the world and one of the best known of Wales's 'Great Little Trains'. In continuous service since 1865, originally to transport slate to the main line at Tywyn down on the coast, its trains now puff merrily to and fro with cargoes of enthusiastic sightseers. The line was saved from obscurity in 1951 by the Talyllyn Railway Preservation Society, the world's first such organisation which has since been emulated by many similar groups. The entire railway

All aboard the Talyllyn

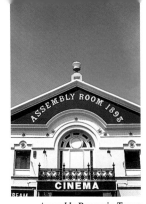

Assembly Rooms in Tywyn

journey of an hour each way can be varied by alighting at intermediate stations. A short walk from Dolgoch Station, for example, leads through woods to the attractive ★ **Dolgoch Falls**; below the falls the line is carried across the little gorge on an impressive viaduct.

Running parallel to the railway, the B4405 meets the A493 at Brynerug, 2 miles (3km) from **Tywyn**, where the railway's main station is situated together with the ★ **Narrow Gauge Railway Museum** (daily 10am–5pm) which combines displays of old locomotives with the history of the slate mining industry in North and Mid Wales. Tywyn's evolution as a seaside resort owed much to John Corbett, a salt baron from Droitwich who built Marine Terrace, the Market Hall and the **Assembly Rooms** (now a cinema). Adjacent to the latter stands **St Cadfan's Church** in which will be found the 7th-century St Cadfan's Stone bearing an inscription thought to be the oldest example of written Welsh in existence.

Maritime Aberdyfi

Dunes seaward of the road and railway extend south to **Aberdyfi (Aberdovey)** – **'Mouth of the Dovey'** – a pleasant resort best known for its golf course and sailing facilities. There is a small **Maritime Museum** at the TIC on The Wharf (daily 10am–1pm, 2pm–6pm; closed end-October to Easter). Started during World War I, it documents the little port's heritage of mineral exports, shipbuilding and seafaring. Aberdyfi boasts a major Outward Bound Centre. A summer ferry plies between here and Ynyslas but the significance of this crossing from North to South Wales diminished with the arrival of the railway and the building of Dyfi Junction Station in 1867. Aberdyfi is also the starting point for the 108-mile (174-km) ★ **Dyfi Valley Walk** exploring countryside on both flanks of the river north to its source under Aran Fawddwy.

Aberdyfi's profile was raised when Charles Dibdin composed the song *The Bells of Aberdovey* for his opera *Liberty Hall* in 1785. Of many stories surrounding the mysteriously pealing bells beneath the sea, the most commonly quoted (and embellished) concerns Cantre'r Gwaelod – the Lowland Hundred. This once fertile low-lying plain was protected from the sea by dykes in the care of Seithennin, a notorious drunkard. One stormy night, while making merry at a feast, he forgot to close the sluices. The Lowland Hundred was inundated and Manua, its principal settlement containing the bells, disappeared forever beneath the waters of Cardigan Bay.

From the top of the village an unclassified road climbs to the route of a prehistoric ridgeway. Ten minutes' walk beyond the farm at the road-end may be found **Carn March Arthur**, a rock bearing the hoofprint of Arthur's horse and marked by a stone tablet. A little further on, down to the left, lies **Llyn Barfog ('Bearded Lake')**, perhaps referring to its covering of water-lilies, or alternatively to various tales of hairy monsters associated with Arthurian legend.

Carn March Arthur

Tracing the Dyfi's shoreline (the National Park boundary) the A493 passes **Pennal.** This could also be reached by taking the mountain road through **Happy Valley**, parallel to the north. Pennal is a very ancient site. At **Cefncaer**, 500m to the southeast, the Romans built a fort guarding one of the lowest crossing points on the Dyfi. Nearby are the mounds of a Bronze Age tumulus and a medieval motte.

At Pen-y-bont turn right over the river and beneath the railway line to enter ★ **Machynlleth**. The town's centrepiece is a splendid **Victorian Clock Tower** built in 1873 to commemorate the Marquess of Londonderry's family who then owned the imposing 17th-century Plas Machynlleth, set in parkland a short distance to the south. The local tourist economy received a boost when the ★★ **Celtica** exhibition (daily 10am–6pm) opened in 1995 in the Plas. Using sophisticated audio-visual technology and imaginative tableaux, it recalls the Celtic influence through 3,000 years of European and specifically Welsh history: as the publicity accurately declares, it is a magical blend of myth and music, landscape and language.

Machynlleth: the clock tower

Facing up to the past at Celtica

Elsewhere in Machynlleth see the 16th-century ★ **Owain Glyndwr Centre** (daily Easter to September 10am–5pm) in the Tourist Information building. It incorporates the remains of an earlier structure in which the Welsh people's hero established the country's first and only (albeit short-lived) Parliament in 1404. George Borrow lodged at the town centre Wynstay Hotel during his tour of Wales in 1854 and was waited on by a 'brisk, buxom maid who told me her name was Mary Evans…'

The Historic Landscape

Prehistoric sites abound in Snowdonia and are particularly common on Anglesey. The earliest inhabitants of the area would have lived by hunting game and gathering shellfish from the shore. During the Neolithic period, from around 3500BC, people learned how to assure a more regular supply of food and lived in settled farming communities around the coast. Using stone axes they cleared areas of forest for cultivation and grazing, and they buried their dead in large chambered tombs like the one at Barclodiad y Gawres near Aberffraw on Anglesey. These burial chambers were distinguished by interior stones incised with mural designs. Other remarkable prehistoric remains can be found inland between Barmouth and Harlech, including the important Dyffryn Cairn at Dyffryn Ardudwy.

The influence of Celtic culture on the historic landscape of Wales began about 700BC. Master metal workers, the Celts produced magnificent objects of intricate design. Their priests and lawmakers were the druids, and above Penmaenmawr stands the Druids Circle associated with the worship of two sinister goddesses, Andras and Ceridwen. Celtic farmsteads have been traced on Anglesey at Ty Mawr near Holyhead, but the best-preserved architectural legacy of the Celts in this part of the world is undoubtedly the 4th-century settlement of Din Lligwy, also on Anglesey (*see Route 2*). Tre'r Ceiri ('Giants' Town'), set on a remote hilltop on the Lleyn Peninsula, is crowded with ancient house sites (*see Route 5*). About 20 are circular and pre-Roman but the majority, some 150 rectangular foundations, represent the complete ground plan of a native town in the Roman period. It was virtually impregnable, with 15ft (4.5m) thick ramparts built between natural rock barriers, and probably flourished as a defensive retreat throughout the entire Roman occupation of Britain.

Ancient settlements: Din Lligwy (above) and Tre'r Ceiri (below)

Following the Roman withdrawal, Christianity fostered the heroic age of the Celtic Church, its missionary saints establishing monastic cells throughout North Wales. During the era of Welsh Princes between the 9th and 13th centuries, Norman abbeys were built at Cymmer, Aberconwy, Cwmhir, Penmon, St Tudwals and Bardsey. Three pilgrimages to Bardsey were worth one to Rome. However, Snowdonia's medieval religious architecture has withstood the rigours of time rather less well than its counterpart in more settled parts of Britain, due mainly to the region's history of struggle and conflict. Nevertheless, in addition to the abbey ruins, notably Penmon on Anglesey (*see Route 2*) and Cymmer near Dolgellau (*see Route 6*), several medieval churches have survived; some, mercifully, have side-stepped the Victorians' often over-

zealous restoration. Good examples are Llanegryn, near Tywyn; Clynnog Fawr, 5 miles (8km) southwest of Caernarfon; and in many out-of-the-way corners across Anglesey and the Lleyn Peninsula.

Snowdonia is synonymous with majestic castles. There are two distinct kinds: 'native' Welsh structures and those built by Edward I following his successful campaigns against the Welsh in the late 13th century. All in the former category were built during the time of Llywelyn the Great and were subsequently strengthened by Edward I after their capture by his troops. Edward's own castles at Conwy, Beaumaris, Caernarfon and Harlech, supported by fortified town walls, demonstrate the best in medieval military architecture. Their often theatrical siting to guard strategic points against Welsh resistance, combined with 'state of the art' defensive design (especially that of Beaumaris, although ironically it never saw military action) would have intimidated any enemy. Even so, all except Caernarfon were taken, if only briefly, by Owain Glyndwr's uprising at the start of the 15th century.

Harlech Castle and Owain Glyndwr

Snowdonia's domestic architecture, while understandably dominated by the sombre tones of granite and slate, does blossom into colourful mode here and there. Behind Aberdyfi's seafront, for instance, lie squares of houses bearing such names as 'The Old Custom House' and 'Liverpool House', built for sea-captains in the 19th century. Caernarfon's 'old town' streets contain several historic taverns. At Conwy are found Jacobean and Georgian houses and the rambling Elizabethan Plas Mawr, built in 1585 by Robert Wynn of Gwydir Castle; recently renovated to a high standard, it is reckoned to be the finest example of its kind in the UK (*see Route 1*).

In many ways slate was to North Wales what coal has been to the South. Terraces of miners' cottages line many a village street in just the same way and tips of spoil have become an accepted part of the landscape. But if the Industrial Revolution left its legacy in Snowdonia primarily as slate mines and quarries (an industrial archaeologist's paradise), smaller sites recall other enterprises. The old winding gear and kilns of Cemaes Brickworks on Anglesey's north coast, for example, belong to an era before roads when heavy commodities were moved by sea. In many locations throughout the region, water-powered woollen mills sprung up to satisfy clothing demands from a growing population. Worthy surviving examples are Trefriw in the Vale of Conwy, Penmachno south of Betws-y-Coed, and Brynkir near Porthmadog.

Two museums with interpretative exhibitions painting broad pictures of the region's history and culture are Oriel Ynys Môn on Anglesey (*see Route 2*) and Oriel Eryri at Llanberis (*see Route 4*).

Legends and Literature

The medieval Welsh story-teller (*y cyfarwydd* – 'the learned one'), like the poet, enjoyed a high social status as court entertainer. He needed a powerful memory and expert narrative techniques to recreate tales and folklore at each performance. The Welsh tradition of oral story-telling is a strong one, continuing down through generations from its origins in the Dark Ages to the modern period. Very little, however, has been preserved. The most important collection of medieval tales – the four branches of the *Mabinogion* – are contained in two texts from around the mid-1300s: the White Book of Rhydderch and the Red Book of Hergest. With its well-told, complex and often moving stories, the *Mabinogion* is arguably Wales's greatest contribution to European literature.

The romanticised, quasi-historical hero, Arthur, features prominently in the Celtic tradition. High up in Cwm Llan under the southern face of Snowdon, treacherous Sir Mordred joined with the Saxon army to end Arthur's reign for good. Wounded at dusk by a chance Saxon arrow, Arthur confronted Mordred on the steep saddle between Snowdon and Lliwedd, and there they fought to their deaths. The pass is still called *Bwlch-y-Saethau* – 'Pass of the Arrows'.

Arthur lives on in legend **63**

The Welsh poet Peter Finch has written that 'to live in Wales is to love sheep and to be afraid of dragons...' Certainly monsters and dragons feature widely in the folklore of Snowdonia, not to mention the Welsh national flag. One legend – a children's favourite – concerns the *afanc* of Glaslyn. Long ago before histories were written, people in the Vale of Conwy were troubled by an enormous beast (*afanc*) whose supernatural powers caused disastrous floods, ruining crops and drowning livestock. Impervious to any weapon forged by man, this dreadful creature resided in a Beaver Pool near Betws-y-Coed. When elders decided to try and remove it to some other distant lake, strong iron chains were forged and two of the mightiest oxen made ready. A courageous damsel lured the *afanc* from its underwater lair (it evidently had a predilection for beautiful maidens), whereupon it was tethered to the oxen and dragged through the parish of Dolwyddelan. Over the shoulder between Moel Siabod and Cribau – *Bwlch Rhiw-yr-Ychain* ('Pass of the Oxen's Slope') – they went, one ox losing an eye with the effort which shed tears to form *Pwll Llygad yr Ych* ('Pool of the Ox's Eye').

Struggling up into Cwm Dyli, past Llyn Llydaw, the exhausted team finally released the *afanc* into the deep waters of Llyn Ffynnon Las ('Lake of the Blue Fountain'), now called Glaslyn. And there he dwells to this day.

Beware the Beast of Glaslyn

Victorian traditions rekindled at the Lloyd George Museum

Folklore, Shows and Festivals

Much of Snowdonia, alluring as it may be to holiday-makers and outdoor enthusiasts, remains essentially rural in character. Although eroded by our increasingly technological society, here and there in farm and village communities customs from a more inter-dependent and superstitious past are kept alive, sometimes for posterity, sometimes out of necessity. For example, co-operative work groups – *cymhorthau* – upon which neighbouring farmers once depended to get big jobs done in this rugged area, continue in the collaboration still required for sheep gathering and the shearing parties. The working skills of sheepdogs and their handlers have developed into competitive trials held during the summer months (details from local TICs). Although most of the dogs used are Border Collies, efforts are being made to re-establish the old Welsh breed before it dies out. Mutual aid and celebration are evident too in the corn harvests of Anglesey and the Caernarfon area. Ornamental harvest-mares, or *caseg fediau*, are made from the last tufts of grain to be cut.

Many hands make light work – particularly at shearing time

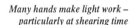

Notable events in the farming calendar include the **North Wales Agricultural Show** held at Caernarfon in July, the **Anglesey County Show** at Llangefni in August, and the **Meirioneth County Agricultural Show**, **Farming Festival** and **Sheepdog Trials**, all held at Dolgellau, also during August.

In years gone by, it was customary for men to present carved **love-spoons** to their intended brides as tokens of their feelings. While the sentimental function may have been lost, Welsh love-spoons are still crafted for gifts and eisteddfod competitions.

The **eisteddfod** dates back to meetings between Celtic bards. The first recorded bardic contest was that of 1176, convened at Cardigan by Rhys ap Gruffydd. It was proclaimed a year and a day in advance (a custom still observed) to ensure high standards; miniature silver chains were presented as prizes for poetry and music. However, the eisteddfod as an important public occasion only became properly established after the Corwen event of 1789. Choral competitions were soon introduced to reflect the growth of chapel choirs. Between 1861 and 1880 the **Royal National Eisteddfod of Wales** was formed to promote worthy cultural standards and to safeguard the Welsh language. The festival is held alternately in North and South Wales during the first week of August and is proclaimed a year and a day in advance at a traditional neo-druidic ceremony within a specially laid out Gorsedd Circle of Stones to the accompaniment of harp music. It is Europe's largest arts and music festival, with a spectacular 9-day programme. Smaller eisteddfodau take place locally, providing marvellous opportunities to see Welsh art and crafts and to hear performances of music, poetry and song.

Eisteddfod performers

Wales is renowned for its **male voice choirs** and this love of singing in harmony extends to chapels and village halls at local concerts and at times of religious and civic celebration. Indeed, it is likely to burst forth spontaneously among groups of friends whatever the occasion.

The main festivals devoted to music and the arts in Snowdonia take place at **Criccieth** in June, **Machynlleth** in August, and **Barmouth** and **Conwy** in September, with the famous **Llangollen International Musical Eisteddfod** spanning six magical days in July each year just to the west of the region along the A5. Also well worth taking in are the **Llandudno Victorian Extravaganza** over the May Day bank holiday weekend, the **International Celtic Festival** at Cemaes in August, and on-going programmes of art exhibitions at **Oriel Mostyn**, Llandudno, and **Oriel Ynys Môn** at Llangefni on Anglesey.

Some other events

April – Snowdonia Classic Vehicle Rally, **Llanberis**, tel: (01286) 870765.

June – Three Peaks Yacht Race start, **Barmouth**, tel: (01341) 280787.

July – Bluegrass Festival, **Conwy**, tel: (01492) 592248; Sesiwn Fawr Folk Festival, **Dolgellau**, tel: (01341) 280787; Caernarfon Festival, tel: (01286) 672232; Snowdon Race, **Llanberis**, tel: (01286) 870765; Regatta and Fun Week, **Barmouth**, tel: (01341) 280787.

August – Menai Straits Regatta, **Beaumaris**, tel: (01248) 352786; Victorian Week, **Tywyn and Talyllyn Railways**, tel: (01654) 710070.

September – National Trust Snowdonia Marathon, **Llanberis**, tel: (01286) 870765.

Food and Drink

Opposite: refreshment at hand in Beddgelert

Allports for fish and chips

North Wales is justly proud of its succulent mountain-bred **lamb** and **black beef**. However, many visitors also savour the region's seafood. The Conwy estuary and Menai Strait, both shallow and strongly tidal, provide ideal conditions for the cultivation of **mussels**, delicious served in a white wine and cream sauce, while the rocky shores around Anglesey and the Lleyn Peninsula yield excellent **oysters**, **crabs** and **lobsters**. For colder days try *cawl*, a traditional meat, root vegetable and leek soup; or perhaps *lobscows*, a warming lamb broth. **Allports** of Porthmadog has been voted Wales's finest fish and chip shop.

Different parts of Snowdonia have their own products: high-quality *rosé* **meat** from the Lleyn and Cadwaladers celebrated **ice-cream**, which originated at Criccieth in the 1920s but is now widely available, being just two examples. Morning coffee and afternoon tea provide excellent opportunities to enjoy **Welsh cakes** (*Cacen Radell*) – they are flat, round, fruited and spread with butter or castor sugar. Another teatime favourite is *Bara Brith*, an old-fashioned fruited tea bread whose equivalent is found in other Celtic countries: *Barm Brack* in Ireland, *Selkirk Bannock* in Scotland, and in Brittany *Morlais Brioche*.

Tempting Welsh cakes

67

The great Liberal politician and statesman David Lloyd George, who relished simple Welsh country fare at his home near Criccieth, had a particular fancy for pig's head brawn, mutton broth with oatcakes, grilled herrings and *Cacen Gri* (another variation on the Welsh cakes theme). Traditional recipes compiled by the Criccieth Women's Institute and first published after World War I included 'Recipes for the Favourite Dishes of the Prime Minister'. The following instructions were for **Steamed Snowdon Pudding**. Mix ¼lb breadcrumbs with ¾oz ground rice or semolina. Stir in 2oz margarine or suet. Next place 2oz raisins in a greased pudding basin with 2 tablespoons of golden syrup. Add 3oz castor sugar to the crumb mixture and blend all ingredients together. Pour into the basin until three-quarters full, cover with greased paper and steam for 2 hours. Serve with custard or marmalade sauce.

Afternoon teas

Light refreshments are provided at innumerable establishments throughout Snowdonia. A selection of the best are: **Pantri Party Cooks** in Pwllheli's West End, widely renowned for home-baked cakes, **The Old Coffee Shop** in New Street, Aberdyfi, built into a rock outcrop; **Plas Café** on Harlech's High Street (closed late October to Easter), a 17th-century town house decorated in 1920s style; **The Pinnacle Café**, Capel Curig, patronised by hungry walkers and cyclists in the heart of northern Snow-

Afternoon in Caernarfon

donia; **Pen y Bryn Tearooms** in Lancaster Square, Conwy (closed winter Mondays), whose proprietor believes 'Visitors to Wales expect things Welsh'; on Bala's High Street **Y Radell ('The Griddle')** in a 17th-century interior adorned with old rural implements; and **Anne's Pantry** at Moelfre on Anglesey, overlooking a quiet cove and serving delicious scones.

Restaurant Selection

The following list, arranged in alphabetical order of placenames, is just a small selection of what Snowdonia offers. For further ideas and locations, consult the local tourist brochures. Establishments providing traditional Welsh food display the Taste of Wales sign – a red dragon on a green background.

Aberdyfi
Penhelig Arms Hotel, tel: (01654) 767215. Old-fashioned country cooking in an 18th-century harbourside inn. Generous portions and excellent wine list. ££

Abersoch
Porth Tocyn Hotel, tel: (01758) 713303. Family-run for 40 years. Fair deal for children. ££

Beaumaris
Ye Olde Bull's Head, tel: (01248) 810329. Restaurant above 15th-century pub near the castle. ££

Capel Garmon
Tan-y-Foel, tel: (01690) 710507. Off-the-beaten-track converted farmhouse. Welsh cuisine. £££

Dolgellau
Dylanwad Da, tel: (01341) 422870. Colourful bistro offering vegetarian choice. ££

Harlech
Castle Cottage, tel: (01766) 780479. Oak-beamed hotel beneath Castle's wing. Excellent value. £

Llanberis
Y Bistro, tel: (01286) 871278. Specialises in local Welsh produce, including lamb, beef and mussels. ££

Llandudno
Bodysgallen Hall, tel: (01492) 582519. Imposing 17th-century fortified mansion set in 200 acres. £££

Portmeirion
Portmeirion Hotel, tel: (01766) 770228. Stunning setting. Contemporary Welsh dishes with Mediterranean influence reflecting Italianate surroundings. ££

Talsarnau
Maes-y-Neuadd, tel: (01766) 780200. Peter Jackson leads Welsh National Culinary Team. Collaborates with Ffestiniog Railway for 'Steam and Cuisine' events. ££

Trefriw
Chandler's, tel: (01492) 640991. Family-run. Separate vegetarian menu. £

Quality in Dolgellau

Al fresco in Betws-y-Coed

Active Holidays

On the boulder-strewn Glyders

Walking

Snowdonia provides scope for pursuing many outdoor activities and sports. By far the most popular is walking. OS maps reveal large concentrations of close-knit contour lines denoting steep ground. This is the domain of hill-walkers for whom there is an almost bewildering choice of routes. There are, however, plenty of guidebooks and leaflets available at information centres and bookshops. Climbing **Snowdon** or **Cadair Idris** are popular goals but their often congested paths are not to everyone's taste.

Each mountain range enjoys its own distinctive character. In the north the **Carneddau** offer vast grassy whale-back ridges, while the adjacent **Glyders** and **Tryfan** are strewn with frost-shattered boulders. Behind Tremadog Bay rise the **Rhinogs**, unfrequented mountains of ankle-twisting rock and deep heather. Both the **Cadair Idris** and **Snowdon** massifs offer rugged walking, sustained gradients and wonderful views. By contrast, the featureless and often boggy **Migneint** between Bala and Ffestiniog is strictly for connoisseurs of solitude. The **Aran ridge** running north from Dinas Mawddwy to Bala Lake is regaining popularity after access problems. West and north of Blaenau Ffestiniog the **Moelwyns** are laced with fascinating relics of slate mining.

For family groups and the less mobile there are miles of gentler footpaths and bridleways to explore. Good examples may be found in **Gwydir Forest** around Betws-y-Coed, in **Coed y Brenin Forest** near Dolgellau and around many of Snowdonia's more accessible **lakes**. The dismantled **Welsh Highland Railway** at Beddgelert gives an entertaining ramble through several tunnels and there is estuary-edge walking on the **Penmaenpool to Morfa Mawddach Track** west of Dolgellau. Sections of the

Route finding at Pen-y-Pass

In the mist on Cadair Idris

Exploring Anglesey's coast

Climber on 'Merlin', Tremadog

Anglesey shoreline possess marvellous coastal paths, notably on the west and north sides of the island, and there are good stretches of path, too, around the tip of the **Lleyn Peninsula**. Then there are the so-called **Precipice Walks**, principally around the Mawddach Estuary, the best known of which starts from from parking near Llyn Cynwch. Precipice Walks are not as hazardous as they might sound, being simply well-made footpaths which, however, traverse very steep hillsides.

Waymarked long-distance trails include the 108-mile (174-km) **Dyfi Valley Way**, the 60-mile (97-km) **North Wales Path** between Prestatyn and Bangor, and the circular 121-mile (194-km) **Anglesey Coast Path**. Of various challenge walks, the most famous is the **Welsh 3000s**, a gruelling 37-mile (60km) tramp over all 14 of Snowdonia's 3,000ft (914m)-plus summits within a 24-hour period. It's not for the faint-hearted.

Details of the Snowdonia National Park's programme of **guided walks** appear in its free visitor newspaper – *Eryri*. Walk leaders invariably have extensive knowledge of the area's history, scenery and people. Routes are graded for difficulty and duration.

It is important to be properly shod and clothed for walking. Even on low-level paths the weather can change quickly, while on the tops protection from the elements may become vital for survival. Since the installation of an automatic, solar-powered weather station on Snowdon summit, with hourly data relayed to base stations by cellphone, reliable **mountain forecasts** are now assured. Tel: (0891) 500449. For a general North Wales weather bulletin, tel: (0891) 505315.

Climbing

Snowdonia's great buttresses and gullies have attracted rock-climbers in ever greater numbers since before World War I when Colin Kirkus and John Menlove Edwards pioneered audacious new ascents. Later, in the 1950s, the likes of Joe Brown and Don Whillans immortalised such locations as the **Llanberis Pass** and Snowdon's **Clogwyn Du'r Arddu**. More recently interest has spread out from the inland crags to embrace the sea cliffs of **Anglesey**, the **Lleyn Peninsula**, Llandudno's **Great Orme** and the cliffs north of **Tremadog**. While it is feasible for confident hillwalkers to tackle scrambling routes (requiring the use of hands as well as feet), aid-climbing with ropes should only be attempted in the company of an experienced companion or a qualified instructor.

Courses in hillwalking, climbing, mountaineering and associated sports, including skiing, are provided at Wales's **National Mountain Centre** at Plas y Brenin, Capel Curig, tel: (01690) 720214.

Mountain Biking

Every kind of cycling terrain exists is the Snowdonia region, from meandering back-lanes to severe mountain gradients. Off-road riding is permitted on public bridleways, unclassified roads and on specially waymarked cycle tracks such as those provided in the **Gwydir** and **Coed y Brenin** forests. Cycling is not permitted on footpaths or over trackless countryside. Under the **National Voluntary Cycling Agreement for Snowdonia**, reached between the cycling organisations, the Sports Council for Wales, Gwynedd County Council and Snowdonia National Park Authority, cyclists are requested not to ride up to, or down from, the summit of Snowdon between 10am and 5pm from 1 June to 30 September. There is full access from October to the end of May. A leaflet available at cycle shops, Warden Centres and Tourist Information Centres outlines alternative routes through mountainous terrain in the Snowdon area. With careful use of an OS map, many worthwhile itineraries 'off the beaten track' can be devised to suit individual abilities. The gentle countryside and quiet country lanes of **Anglesey** and the **Lleyn Peninsula** make them ideal for family cycling.

On Anglesey's quiet lanes

Sailing off Beaumaris

Other Activities

You do not have to be an expert to enjoy **pony-trekking**. Trekking centres will match horses to individual riding ability; the pace is relaxed and younger children can go along too. **Riding** and **hacking** are for the more experienced, with **trail riding**, sometimes over several days, the most adventurous option. **Welsh mountain ponies** and the smaller **Welsh cobs** are used at most riding/trekking centres. Access to the countryside is virtually the same as for mountain biking. The main regional centres are situated at **Penmaenpool**, near Dolgellau, tel: (01341) 422377; **Waunfawr**, near Caernarfon, tel: (01286) 650342; **Llanfairfechan**, tel: (01248) 681143; **Ty Coch Farm** near Penmachno, tel: 01690 760248; and **Dwyran** on Anglesey, tel: (01248) 430977.

Pony-trekking near Penmaenpool

Snowdonia's long coastline bordering Cardigan Bay and the Irish Sea is a premier venue for **dinghy sailing**. There are excellent marinas at **Conwy**, **Caernarfon** and **Pwllheli**, as well as numerous sheltered moorings in fishing harbours and bays. **Surfing**, **windsurfing** and **sea-kayaking** are catered for by a coast offering exposure to, or protection from, all points of the compass. For more information contact the **National Watersports Centre for Wales** at Plas Menai. Tel: (01248) 670964.

Inland, **canoeing** is enjoyed on mountain lakes and challenging rivers. For suitable locations and prevailing conditions contact the **National White Water Centre** near Bala, tel: (01678) 521083.

The National White Water Centre

71

Getting There

Opposite: driving in past Tall-y-Llyn Lake

By ship

There are ferry services between Holyhead, Dun Laoghaire and Dublin, including a high-speed car carrying catamaran. Stena Line, tel: (0990) 707070; Irish Ferries, tel: (0990) 329129.

By train

The main London Euston to Holyhead service stops at Llandudno Junction and Bangor. Other local trains call at Conwy, Penmaenmawr, Llanfairfechan and all stations on Anglesey. Blaenau Ffestiniog is reached by a branch line through the Vale of Conwy from Llandudno Junction. From Blaenau Ffestiniog the narrow-gauge Ffestiniog Railway runs down to Porthmadog, connecting at Minffordd station with the scenic Cambrian Coast Line between Pwllheli and Aberystwyth. Services to and from the Midlands via Shrewsbury and Machynlleth connect with the Cambrian Coast Line at Dovey Junction. For all timetable and fare enquiries, tel: (0345) 484950.

On the platform at Blaenau Ffestiniog

73

By car

Access from the northwest has been greatly speeded up by completion of the A55 North Wales Expressway which continues beneath the Conwy estuary to Bangor and (when completed) Holyhead. For the Vale of Conwy, Betws-y-Coed and The Vale of Ffestiniog, take the southbound A470 from Glan Conwy. Thomas Telford's London to Holyhead highway, now the A5, heads west from the M54 via Llangollen to Capel Curig and thence through the mountains to Bethesda and the A55.

Motoring into Caenarfon

Befitting its Roman origins, Caernarfon sits at the hub of radiating roads. The A4085 and A4086 flank Snowdon itself while the A495 strikes southwest for the Lleyn Peninsula. Two good parallel north-south roads link the Vale of Ffestiniog with the River Mawddach, taking in the Cardigan Bay resorts and Coed-y-Brenin Forest.

Southwest from Bala towards Dolgellau the A494 follows a major geological fault line; it continues as the B4405, skirting Cadair Idris to reach the coast at Tywyn. Southeastern Snowdonia is approached on the A470 from Llanidloes and Newtown, or the A458 from Shrewsbury.

By coach

National Express operate services to Llandudno, Bangor, Caernarfon and Porthmadog from London and Manchester, tel: (0990) 808080. Crosville Wales provide the 'Traws-Cambria' (trans-Wales) services from South Wales to Dolgellau, Porthmadog, Caernarfon and Bangor, tel: (01492) 592111.

Waiting for the Sherpa at Pen-y-Pass

Talyllyn timetable and train

Getting Around

By bus and train

Snowdonia enjoys an excellent network of buses, including the Snowdon Sherpa, a circular service around the northern part of the region giving access to the mountains and main towns (reduced winter timetable). There are currently over 20 independent bus operators; for local journeys enquire at a TIC. Red Rover bus tickets give a limitless day's travelling on any buses in Gwynedd, Conwy and Snowdon Sherpa timetables (but not on coaches or trains). North and Mid Wales Rover tickets, available from all railway stations, allow unlimited travel on trains and buses during their period of validity.

Regional Railways services across Anglesey, through the Vale of Conwy, down the Cardigan Bay coast and inland to Machynlleth, provide a relaxed and 'green' way to enjoy the scenery. Combined with bus routes, narrow-gauge railways and with some careful planning, much of Snowdonia is accessible without a car. For enquiries about public transport in Gwynedd tel: (01286) 679535; in Conwy tel: (01492) 575414. Gwynedd Public Transport Maps and Timetables, available free from National Park Centres and libraries, are a useful source of information.

Maps

Six Ordnance Survey Landranger maps are needed for complete coverage of the Snowdonia region at a scale of 1:50,000. They are: 115 for Snowdon, 114 for Anglesey, 123 for the Lleyn Peninsula, 124 for Porthmadog and Cadair Idris, 125 for Bala, and 135 for Aberdyfi and Machynlleth. Outdoor Leisure maps (1:25,000) cover Snowdon and Conwy Valley areas (Sheet 17), Harlech and Bala areas (Sheet 18) and Cadair Idris area (Sheet 23).

Facts for the Visitor

Tourist Information

For more information about visiting Snowdonia, contact either a National Park Centre or a local Tourist Information Centre.

Snowdonia National Park Information Service, Penrhyndeudraeth, tel: (01766) 770274.

National Park Centres: Aberdyfi, tel: (01654) 767321; **Betws-y-Coed**, tel: (01690) 710426; **Blaenau Ffestiniog**, tel: (01766) 830360; **Dolgellau**, tel: (01341) 422888; **Harlech**, tel: (01766) 780658.

National Park Information points are at Beddgelert, Capel Garmon, Fron-goch, Llanfachreth, Llanuwchllyn, Llwyngwril, Maentwrog, Mallwyd, Pennal, Talybont (Conwy Valley), Talybont (Harlech), and Ysbyty Ifan.

A ubiquitous sign

Tourist Information Centres contain a wide range of leaflets and publications, many of them free. As well as answering public transport enquiries, staff will usually help arrange accommodation. Suggestions for eating out, places to visit and details of local events are also offered. **Aberdyfi**: Wharf Gardens, tel: (01654) 767321; **Abersoch**: tel: (01758) 712929; **Bala**: Pensarn Road, tel: (01678) 521021; **Barmouth**: Station Road, tel: (01341) 280787; **Betws-y-Coed**: The Stables, tel: (01690) 710426; **Blaenau Ffestiniog**: High Street, tel: (01766) 830360; **Caernarfon**: Oriel Pendeitsh, Castle Street, tel: (01286) 672232; **Conwy**: Castle Entrance, tel: (01492) 592248; **Corris**: Craft Centre, tel: (01654) 761244; **Dolgellau**: Eldon Square, tel: (01341) 422888; **Harlech**: High Street, tel: (01766) 780658; **Holyhead**: Turkey Shore Road, tel: (01407) 762622; **Llanberis**: 41a High Street, tel: (01286) 870765; **Llanfairpwllgwyngyll**: Station Site, tel: (01248) 713177; **Llandudno**: 1–2 Chapel Street, tel: (01492) 876413; **Porthmadog**: High Street, tel: (01766) 512981; **Pwllheli**: Sgwar yr Orsaf, tel: (01758) 613000; **Tywyn**: High Street, tel: (01654) 710070.

Souvenirs

Traditional crafts can be found in numerous outlets throughout Snowdonia. Mill shops such as those at Trefriw, Penmachno and Brynkir display woven fabrics and garments made on the premises using **Welsh wool**. Carved to make gifts and useful items, **slate** is a popular souvenir; it is available at craft shops and at such visitor attractions as the Inigo Jones Slateworks near Caernarfon and Blaenau Ffestiniog's slate mines. **Portmeirion pottery** is well regarded and widely collected; it can be purchased from Portmeirion and other quality gift shops. Examples of **working potteries** are Snowdon Mill, Porthmadog, and

SIOP
ʒwaɪtʜ
aʒ
ORIEl

FACTORY
shop
aɴɒ
ʒallERY

Crafts outlet in Beddgelert

Island Pottery at Llanrhuddlad on Anglesey. Other crafts are practised and on sale at **Corris Craft Centre** between Dolgellau and Machynlleth.

Market Days
Sunday: Harlech
Monday: Dolgellau
Tuesday: Blaenau Ffestiniog
Wednesday: Machynlleth, Pwllheli
Thursday: Bala, Barmouth, Llangefni
Friday: Porthmadog
Saturday: Bangor, Conwy

Market day in Pwllheli

Medical
There are doctors' surgeries in all the main towns. The region's principal hospital is at Bangor.

Emergencies
Dial 999 and ask the operator for the appropriate service, ie: Police, Ambulance, Fire Brigade, Coastguard or Mountain Rescue. (NB: Mountain rescue call-outs are initiated by the Police)

At the newsagent in Bala

Newspapers
Northern Snowdonia interest is served by the North Wales Weekly News, published in Llandudno Junction. Topics in southern Snowdonia are covered by the Cambrian News, published in Aberystwyth. The Daily Post is distributed throughout the region.

Language
Because Welsh occurs for place-names and natural features throughout Snowdonia, the following brief Glossary is included, plus some other useful words and phrases.

aber – mouth of a river
afon – river
bach/fach – small
bore da – good morning
bryn – hill
bwlch – pass
caer – fort
capel – chapel
carreg – stone
castell – castle
coch – red
coed – forest
craig – rock
croes/groes – cross
croeso – welcome
cwm – valley or hollow

Cymru – Wales
dinas – fortification
diolch yn fawr – thank you
drws – pass
du/ddu – black
dyffryn – vale
eglwys – church or in the parish of
fawr/mawr – large
ffordd – road
ffridd – mountain pasture
ffynnon – spring
foel/moel – rounded hill
gwynt – wind
hen – old
llan – church

llyn – lake
melin/felin – mill
morfa – coastal marsh
mynydd – mountain
nant – valley or stream
newydd – new
nos da – goodnight
pentre – village
pistyll – waterfall
plas – mansion
rhaeadr – waterfall
traeth – shore or beach
y – the
ynys – island
ysbyty – hospital
ysgol – school

Snowdonia for Children

Few palces in Britain have such an abundance of visitor attractions as Snowdonia. Most of these are suitable for children and have been described in the main Places section of this guide. They include the region's **Great Little Trains**, such as the Snowdon Mountain Railway (*see Route 4*), the Tallyllyn Railway (*see Route 9*), the Bala Lake Railway (*see Route 7*) and the Ffestiniog Railway (*see Route 3*); its **slate caverns** at Blaenau Ffestiniog (*see Route 3*); its **underground power stations** (*see Routes 3 and 4*); and its **historical museums** such as the much-acclaimed **Celtica** in Machynlleth (*see Route 9*). Then there are all the castles, the **Centre for Alternative Technology** (CAT, *see Route 8*) and **King Arthur's Labyrinth** (*see also Route 8*) – the list goes on.

Down the Llechwedd Caverns (above) and at the CAT (below)

Snowdonia National Parks provide a programme of **guided walks** between March and September each year. Many are suitable for the whole family or for older children on their own. The walks are graded from 'very easy/flat' to 'stamina required/mostly on high ground'. Details can be found in the free National Park newspaper – *Eryri* – or by calling the National Park Offices, tel: (01766) 770274.

During the summer holiday season, Plas y Brenin – Wales's National Mountain Centre – runs **Taster Sessions** for youngsters. On any weekday they can choose a 2-hour period practising either **climbing/abseiling**, **skiing** or **canoeing**. Alternatively, parents can drop their children off for a whole day's instruction in all three activities. For details, tel: (01690) 720214.

Pony trekking is widely available too; contact local TIC's for details. Centres displaying the British Horse Society's logo have been inspected. Most **mountain bike** hire centres cater for youngsters and family groups and will provide guidance on which trails are suitable.

The National Trust holds **fun days** for children during the summer at some of their properties, notably Penrhyn Castle near Bangor. Events there range from Woodland Wildlife with Trusty the Hedgehog and an educational Victorian Childhood Experience, to Beatrix Potter and Famous Five Adventures. For details contact the National Trust, tel: (01492) 860123.

Anglesey is particularly well endowed with specifically child-orientated attractions. Fossils, dinosaur bones, rocks and minerals are explored at **Stone Science** near Llangefni. **Archery**, woodland **den building** and **stilt walking** are some of the activities at the Greenwood Centre. There are exotic birds and **birds of prey** at Bird World, and **farm animals** to feed and learn about at Foel and Bryntirion farms. Anglesey also boasts a good **Sea Zoo**.

Anglesey Sea Zoo

Accommodation

Hotels and guest houses

The Pen-y-Gwryd Hotel

A wide selection of serviced accommodation is on offer, from clean, modest guest houses to luxury hotels with every amenity. Typical prices for B&B in a guest house range from around £13 to £23; in a hotel from around £16 to £80 depending on specifications. Pubs often provide overnight accommodation too, ranging from around £15 to £30 for B&B. Many establishments serve evening meals (dinner) as an optional extra. Some will provide packed lunches; vegetarian and vegan menus may sometimes be available. There may also be special reductions for children or Senior Citizens. TICs hold details of local accommodation and will help with bookings.

Self-catering

Self-catering cottages, farmhouses, flats, chalets and static caravans are numerous. Low season weekly tariffs from as little as £80 represent good value, although in the peak season (when advance booking is essential) weekly rentals rise to £300 or more depending on the unit's size and location. Short breaks are widely available at attractive prices. One of the specialist self-catering agencies is Wales Holidays, Bear House, Broad Street, Newtown, Powys SY16 2QZ, tel: (01686) 628200. There are many excellent campsites in Snowdonia, usually costing between £5 and £8 for an overnight pitch.

The Swallow Falls Hotel

Area by Area

The following short list samples various types of accommodation for overnight stays or longer holidays.

Llandudno
Winston Guest House, tel: (01492) 876144. Home cooking. 5 mins from pier and shops. **St George's Hotel**, tel: (01492) 877544. Grand Victorian seafront hotel with all amenities. **The Lighthouse**, tel: (01492) 876819. Sensational location on Great Ormes Head.

Vale of Conwy
Glan Heulog, Conwy, tel: (01492) 593845. Warm welcome; close to Conwy Castle. **Church House**, Llanbedr-y-Cennin, tel: (01492) 660521. Listed 16th-century building in hillside village. **Swallow Falls Hotel**, Betwsy-Coed, tel: (01690) 710796. Home-cooked food in tavern bar; landscaped gardens opposite famous waterfall.

Around Snowdon
Llugwy Guest House, Capel Curig, tel: (01690) 720218. Established over 100 years. Good touring base. **Pen-y-**

Llugwy Guest House

Gwryd Hotel, Nantgwynant, tel: (01286) 870211. Traditional hostelry, one-time base for Everest expedition training. **Sygun Fawr Country House Hotel**, Beddgelert, tel: (01766) 890258. 17th-century Welsh manor house. Ideal base for walking. **Gallt-y-Glyn Hotel**, Llanberis, tel: (01286) 870370. Snowdon views. Vegetarian and special diets. **Prince of Wales Hotel**, Caernarfon, tel: (01286) 674602. Splendid Welsh cuisine, close to castle.

Anglesey
Plas Llangaffo Farmhouse, Llangaffo, tel: (01248) 440452. Pets and children welcome. Vegetarian choice available. **Drws-y-Coed**, Llannerch-y-medd, tel: (01248) 470473. Peaceful location on 550-acre working farm, central Anglesey. Well appointed historic farmstead.

Lleyn Peninsula
Tyddyn Iolyn, Pentrefelin, Criccieth, tel: (01766) 522509. 16th-century farmhouse. Chickens, cats, ducks and pony. **Ty Draw Guest House**, Abersoch, tel: (01758) 712647. Offers helpful maps and guides to the area. Fantastic breakfasts. **Caeau Capel Hotel**, Nefyn, tel: (01758) 720240. Family hotel in own grounds with putting green.

Ty Draw Guest House

Tremadog Bay and Vale of Ffestiniog.
Portmeirion Hotel, Portmeirion, tel: (01766) 770228. Magical setting in Italianate village overlooking Dwryd estuary. **Afallon**, Blaenau Ffestiniog, tel: (01766) 830468. Homely Welsh welcome. Reduced rates for children. **Godre'r Graig**, Harlech, tel: (01766) 780905. Adjacent to castle. Vegetarian choice. Mountain bikes for hire.

A favourite in Blaenau

Cardigan Bay resorts
Plas Bach Country Guest House, Bontddu, Barmouth, tel: (01341) 281234. Georgian house above Mawddach estuary. **Cynfal Farm**, Bryncrug, Tywyn, tel: (01654) 711703. Talyllyn Railway runs through this working farm. Magnificent views. **The Harbour Hotel**, Aberdyfi, tel: (01654) 767250. Family hotel on the waterfront.

Southern Snowdonia
Melin Meloch, Bala, tel: (01678) 520101. 15th-century water mill with working Victorian turbine. En-suite rooms in Granary and Miller's Cottage; meals in Mill House. **The Dolbrodmaeth Inn**, Dinas Mawddwy, tel: (01650) 531333. Egon Ronay menu, salmon fishing. **Royal Ship Hotel**, Dolgellau, tel: (01341) 422209. Central location, family rooms, traditional draught ales. **Mathafarn**, Machynlleth, tel: (01650) 511226. Elegant 16th-century country house on working farm. Henry VII stayed here before the Battle of Bosworth.

Index